NUT**SHELLS**

KT-142-687

Equity & Trusts

YOU'VE GOT IT
CRACKED

NUT**SHELLS**

Equity & Trusts

EIGHTH EDITION

by
MICHAEL HALEY, Solicitor, Professor of Law
Keele University
Based on original text by Angela Sydenham

SWEET & MAXWELL

 THOMSON REUTERS

First Edition – 1987
Reprinted 1988
Reprinted 1990
Second Edition – 1991
Third Edition 1994
Reprinted 1996
Fourth Edition – 1997
Fifth Edition – 2000
Reprinted 2002
Reprinted 2003
Sixth Edition 2004
Seventh Edition 2007

Published in 2010 by Thomson Reuters (Legal) Limited
(Registered in England & Wales, Company No 1679046.
Registered Office and address for service:
100 Avenue Road, London NW3 3PF)
trading as Sweet & Maxwell

*For further information on our products and services,
visit www.sweetandmaxwell.co.uk*

Typeset by LBJ Typesetting Ltd of Kingsclere
Printed in Great Britain by Ashford Colour Press, Gosport, Hants

*No natural forests were destroyed to make this product;
only farmed timber was used and re-planted.*

A CIP catalogue record for this book is available from the British Library.

ISBN 978–0–41404–177–6

Thomson Reuters and the Thomson Reuters logo are trademarks of Thomson Reuters.
Sweet & Maxwell® is a registered trademark of Thompson Reuters (Legal) Limited

Contents

Using this Book

Welcome to our new look **NUTSHELLS** revision series. We have revamped and improved the existing design and layout and added new features, according to student feedback.

NEW DETAILED TABLE OF CONTENTS
for easy navigation.

Contents

**REDESIGNED TABLES OF CASES
AND LEGISLATION** for easy reference.

Table of Cases

NEW CHAPTER INTRODUCTIONS
to outline the key concepts covered
and condense complex and important
information.

An Introduction to E

INTRODUCTION

This book considers the doctrines and reme
by the branch of law known as "equity" a
concept of the trust. In particular, t
to equity and trusts and lo
of English

**DEFINITION CHECKPOINTS,
EXPLANATION OF KEY CASES**
to highlight important information.

REMEDIES

terim injunctions

DEFINITION CHECKPOINT

Although an application for summary judgme
IPR proprietor, an interim injunction can ofter
remedy to an IP rightholder. This and the fact
disputes do not progress beyond the interim
by the old terminology—"interlocutory st
injunctions are particularly important in IP

standard guidance as to when an int
in American Cyanamid v Eth

struction under oath.
warded in interim proceedings.
this remedy can be ordered against an,
that the patent is inextricably entwined.

KEY CASE

KIRIN-AMGEN INC V TRANSKARYOTIC THEARAPIES
In *Kirin-Amgen Inc v Transkaryotic Theara*
cells carrying small amounts of patented prote
delivery up.

(c) Court order for a party to reveal relev
Procedure Rules (rule 31) such an ord
example, the name and addre
th the tradition?

DIAGRAMS, FLOWCHARTS AND OTHER DIAGRAMMATIC REPRESENTATION to clarify and condense complex and important information and break up the text.

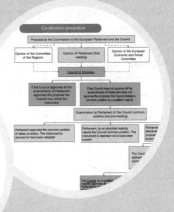

END OF CHAPTER REVISION CHECKLISTS outlining what you should now know and understand.

END OF CHAPTER QUESTION AND ANSWER SECTION with advice on relating knowledge to examination performance, how to approach the question, how to structure the answer, the pitfalls (and how to avoid them!) and how to get the best marks.

QUESTION AND ANSWER

Sample Problem Question

James sells a revolutionary toilet bowl, "t̶
ing remaining permanently white. The toi̶
and are comprised of a perfectly circular c̶
cal brushing made of plastic bumps on ƒ̶
market share of the high end toilet p̶
ᴬale advertising campaign. After h̶
ᴠishes to register a UK t̶

HANDY HINTS
—revision and examination tips and advice relating to the subject features at the end of the book.

HANDY HINTS

The golden rule for most law examinations w̶
all of the question (i.e. all its constituent par̶
(i.e. do not digress, keep your answer relevan̶
revision, practice and planning all have a role̶
    Some issues may require discussion c̶
questions may involve breach of confidence i̶
also require consideration of passing off.

Preparation
    ᴵP examinations require ca̶
        ᵐᵃᵗ and st̶

NEW COLOUR CODING throughout to help distinguish cases and legislation from the narrative. At the first mention, cases are highlighted in colour and italicised and legislation is highlighted in colour and emboldened.

ᵗⁱᵉⁿᵈ to featureᵔ
ᵔ₅es (*Ocular Science v Aspec̶*
interface with a socket would also b̶
See also *Dyson Ltd v Qualtex Ltd* (2004,̶

(iii) "Must match" designs are excluded, *i.e.* c̶
"features of shape or configuration which are̶
ance of another article of which the article ̶
to form an integral part" (**CDPA 1988**, s.21̶
features which need to be made in a certain̶
will be excluded (e.g. see *Mark Wilkinson Fur̶*
(1998). See also *Dyson Ltd v Qualtex Ltd* (20C̶
also be excluded under "must match".

(iv) Surface decoration (**CDPA 1988**, s.213(̶
subsist in surface decoration such as a pair̶
of an article (*Mark Wilkinson Furniture̶*

ᵗ fit" and "must match" e̶

Table of Cases

Table of Statutes

An Introduction to Equity

INTRODUCTION

This book considers the doctrines and remedies which have been developed by the branch of law known as "equity" and places particular emphasis upon the concept of the trust. In particular, this opening chapter serves as an introduction to equity and trusts and looks at the impact that equity has had upon the development of English law.

"Equity" is a term that invokes notions of good conscience, fairness and justice. In modern times, it exerts an influence in every aspect of the civil law and this is particularly so in contract, tort and land law. "Equity" is the branch of law that was administered in the Court of Chancery prior to the **Judicature Acts 1873 and 1875**. This was a jurisdiction evolved to achieve justice and to overcome the rigours and deficiencies of the common law. Injustice was especially apparent in the common law writ system which, put simply, entailed that, if there was no writ, there was no cause of action upon which a claimant could rely. In such instances, the aggrieved party might apply to the King for justice. The King, in turn, passed on these appeals to the Lord Chancellor. In time, the Lord Chancellor developed his own court, the Court of Chancery. Initially, the Court of Chancery operated in a flexible manner in the dispensation of justice. Inevitably, however, equity developed its own body of rules that had, by the nineteenth century, become almost as technical and rigid as those at common law.

FUSION?

Not surprisingly, a dual system of courts proved to be expensive, cumbersome and inconvenient. It also produced major conflict between the common law judges and their chancery counterparts. The **Judicature Acts 1873 and 1875** addressed these issues and provided that all courts could now exercise both a common law and equitable jurisdiction. While the Acts merged the Court of Chancery with the common law courts (to form the Supreme Court of Judicature), Parliament did not fuse the two streams of law. The Acts did establish, however, the supremacy of equity by providing that, in a conflict between law and equity, equitable rules were to prevail. As will become clear, the major differences between the two streams of law concern the types of claim made by litigants and the remedies that are awarded by the court.

EQUITY'S IMPACT

There are many and varied contributions to the substantive law that have been made by equity. The following provide the major examples:

- the trust (originally called a "use"). If property was conveyed to "A upon trust for B", the common law courts regarded A as the absolute owner and would not recognise B's rights. Equity, however, would enforce the trust and compel A (as trustee) to hold the property on behalf of B (the beneficiary);

Figure 1: The Trust

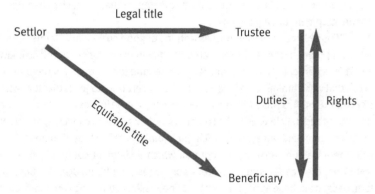

- **restrictive covenants.** The general rule at common law is that covenants only bind the parties themselves and cannot bind third parties. Although the benefit of a covenant can easily be transferred to a third party expressly or under statute (e.g. the Contracts (Rights of Third Parties) Act 1999), stricter rules govern its burden. In relation to freehold covenants affecting land, equity stepped in to allow restrictive (or negative) covenants to run with the land so as to bind all future purchasers;
- **the mortgagor's equitable right to redeem.** Where a landowner mortgages his land (i.e. offers the land as security for a loan), the mortgage contract will specify a contractual date for redemption. This is the agreed date when the debt is to be paid off (redeemed) by the borrower. At common law, the borrower had to discharge the loan by this date or he would lose the land. Equity intervened and allowed repayment to be made even though the contractual date had passed;
- **the subpoena.** This is an order developed by the Court of Chancery to compel a litigant to appear in person before the court and to be questioned;

- **estoppel.** An estoppel arises most commonly in circumstances where X makes a statement, promise or some other representation to Y and, as a result, Y acts to his detriment. Y's detrimental reliance/change of position can trigger an estoppel that will prevent X from enforcing his strict legal rights. Of the various categories of estoppel that exist, the most commonly found are promissory estoppel and proprietary estoppel. Promissory estoppel can only be employed as a defence (it is a shield and not a sword) and hinges upon there being a promise as to future conduct (not existing fact). Proprietary estoppel requires a representation or understanding (whether in the present or future tense) concerning land and can be used as a cause of action (i.e. it confers a positive right to sue);

New Remedies

At common law, the usual remedy is the award of damages and this is available as of right. A wider range of remedies was introduced by equity. These include **specific performance, injunctions, rectification** (rewriting of a contract), **rescission** (unilateral withdrawal from a contract) and the **appointment of a receiver** (to receive income from a business). Until the **Chancery Amendment Act 1858**, however, equity could not award damages for breach of contract. The Act (now in its modern form of s.50 of the **Supreme Court Act 1981**) allowed an award of damages in addition to, or in substitution for, an injunction or specific performance. A distinguishing feature of all equitable remedies is that they are discretionary (i.e. not available as of right) and appropriate only where financial compensation is inadequate. The remedies of specific performance and injunction are considered in more detail below.

THE MAXIMS OF EQUITY

| DEFINITION CHECKPOINT |

There are a number of maxims that represent the general principles of equity. These maxims retain importance because they provide broad guidelines by which the courts exercise their equitable jurisdiction. They should always be borne in mind because, as equitable remedies are discretionary, they may often dictate when (and when not) a remedy will be granted. Below is a list of the most important equitable maxims.

Equity Will Not Suffer a Wrong Without a Remedy

This maxim is not to be taken literally as equitable remedies are geared only to strike against unconscionable behaviour and operate only if that behaviour constitutes a legal (as opposed to a moral) wrongdoing. The law of trusts provides a good illustration, as equity (but not the common law) allows the beneficiary to enforce his rights. A further example concerns injunctions which can be employed to prevent an anticipated wrong, whereas there is no remedy at common law until the wrongful act has been performed. Other modern developments include the evolution of promissory estoppel, the employment of the constructive trust and the expansion of the range of injunctions.

He who Seeks Equity must do Equity

This focuses upon the future conduct of the claimant and entails that, for example, if the claimant seeks to rescind (i.e. withdraw from) a contract, the court will ensure that the claimant acts equitably by returning any deposit paid under the contract. Similarly, if the claimant seeks to specifically enforce a contract then he must be prepared to perform his side of the bargain. If the claimant cannot, or will not, perform his obligations, the court will not grant equitable relief. The maxim is, therefore, employed to ensure fairness.

He who Comes to Equity must come with Clean Hands

This looks to the past conduct of the claimant and entails that, if the claimant's conduct in relation to the dispute has been improper, the chances are that equity will not assist him. For example, specific performance will not be granted in relation to a contract which was brought about by the claimant's misrepresentation or fraud (*Cross v Cross* (1983)) or where the claimant is himself in breach of that contract. If it were otherwise, equity would be operating a dual standard.

Delay Defeats Equity

"Laches" is an example of the operation of this maxim and means that a claimant who takes too long to exercise his legal rights will not receive the assistance of equity. Equity aids the vigilant and not the indolent. The idea is that the claimant has to act expeditiously. In practice, the role of this maxim has been subsumed by the Limitation Act 1987 (which sets out time limits within which actions must be commenced), but as in *Leaf v International Galleries* (1950) it still exerts influence when deciding whether equitable remedies should be granted.

Equity is Equality

This maxim applies where two or more persons claim to be interested in the same property. If their respective shares are not stated, and there is an absence of a contrary intention, equity assumes that they are to have equal shares. For example, as regards claims to property under a fixed trust, if the shares are not allocated between the claimants, equity presumes that each was intended to have an equal share: *Burrough v Philcox* (1840).

Equity will Not Assist a Volunteer

Equity will not grant specific performance of a gratuitous promise (i.e. an agreement that is not supported by consideration). In relation to trusts, this means that equity will assist a beneficiary only when there is a perfectly constituted trust (i.e. once legal title to the trust property has vested in the trustee). This is considered further in Chapter 4.

Equity Looks on That as Done That Ought to Be Done

> **KEY CASE**
>
> **WALSH V LONSDALE**
> In *Walsh v Lonsdale* (1882), a seven-year lease was granted to the tenant, but no deed was executed. The fixed term lease was, therefore, equitable. In the light that specific performance of the contract to create a legal lease was available, the court admitted that an equitable lease is as good as a legal lease. This was because equity looked on the lease as "legal" as soon as it was informally created.

A further example of this maxim is the doctrine of conversion that arises on a binding contract for the sale of land. As soon as the contract is entered, the vendor becomes the trustee of the legal estate for the benefit of the purchaser. This entails that the vendor's interest has been "converted" into the agreed proceeds of sale. Accordingly, if the property is damaged after the contract, the risk potentially falls on the shoulders of the purchaser and the vendor is entitled to the full purchase price.

Equity will Not Permit a Statute to be Used as an Engine of Fraud

This prevents a party from relying upon an absence of statutory formalities (e.g. relating to land contracts, the creation of legal leases and express trusts and the registration of land charges) if to do so would be unconscionable and unfair.

Illustrative cases

- In *Shah v Shah* (2001), a deed was not properly executed and a witness to the deed sought to have it set aside for his own benefit. The court held that for the witness to rely on this defect would be tantamount to fraud and upheld the deed.
- In *Bannister v Bannister* (1948), an elderly woman conveyed a house on the understanding that she would be able to continue to reside there rent free. The bargain was not enforceable by her. Nevertheless, equity

stepped in to prevent injustice and imposed a constructive trust which gave her a life interest in the property.

Equity Acts in Personam

A key feature of equity is that it acts in personam, which means that it is designed to prevent a specified individual from acting unconscionably. It strikes at the conduct and conscience of the defendant. This means that equitable remedies are personal in that they are exercised against specific persons. They compel or permit a person to do something or not to do something. For example, in relation to a breach of trust, the remedy is exercisable against the trustees personally. This can involve an order freezing the trustees' assets even if those assets are subject to a foreign jurisdiction. The maxim also entails that an individual who does not comply with an order of the court will be held to be in contempt and may be imprisoned until he purges his contempt. It also justifies how equity can make an order relating to property situated outside the jurisdiction, provided that the defendant is within the jurisdiction: *Penn v Lord Baltimore* (1750).

Equity Imputes an Intention to Fulfil an Obligation

This means that where a person is obliged to do something, but instead does something else that could be regarded as a performance of the obligation, equity will regard this as fulfilling the obligation. For example, when a debtor leaves a legacy by will to his creditor, the presumption is that the legacy will be viewed as the satisfaction of the debt. The creditor will, therefore, not be able both to sue on the debt and keep the legacy.

Equity will Not Perfect an Imperfect Gift

In order to make a perfect gift the donor must comply with the requirements necessary to transfer legal title to the property. There are numerous examples where equity has not interfered when, although a transfer was intended, the transferor did not follow the appropriate transfer process. In *Jones v Lock* (1865), a father intended to make a gift of a cheque to his child, but failed to endorse the cheque with the result that legal title did not pass. Equity refused to cure the defect and the gift failed. This rule, however, has its exceptions and these include deathbed gifts, fortuitous vesting, proprietary estoppel, unconscionability and the so-called every effort rule. These are considered in Chapter 4.

SPECIFIC PERFORMANCE

DEFINITION CHECKPOINT

Specific performance is, put simply, a court order requiring a party to a contract to perform his side of a contractual bargain.

General Principles

This remedy will not be granted if damages would adequately compensate the claimant. An example of where specific performance will be readily granted concerns contracts for the sale of land. This is because each piece of land is considered to be unique and damages would not compensate the potential purchaser. An action for a specific performance, moreover, may be commenced even before there has been an actual breach of contract. This would arise where there is an anticipatory breach (e.g. one party states that he will not perform the contract): see *Hasham v Zenab* (1960).

Restricted availability

Specific performance is not available for all types of contract. It does not cover, for example:

- most contracts for the sale of goods, unless they are unique (*Behnke v Bede Shipping Co* (1927): a ship); special circumstances make the payment of damages inadequate (*Sky Petroleum Ltd v VIP Petroleum Ltd* (1974): sale of petrol at a time of world shortage) or catered for by statutory provision (e.g. the Sale of Goods Act 1979 relates to the performance of "specific or ascertained goods");
- illegal or immoral contracts (e.g. a contract to pay for stolen goods) or when the specific performance of the contract would offend public policy. In *Wroth v Tyler* (1974) the order was refused because it would cause a husband to sue a wife with whom he was still residing;
- agreements where there is no consideration ("equity will not assist a volunteer");
- contracts for transient interests (e.g. a tenancy at will) because "equity will not act in vain". Specific performance may, however, be available to enforce contractual licences where damages are an inadequate remedy (*Verrall v Great Yarmouth* (1981));
- contracts requiring continuous supervision e.g. a contract to provide porterage in a block of flats (*Ryan v Mutual Tontine Westminster Chambers Association* (1893)) and a covenant to keep open a business in a shopping centre (*Co-operative Insurance Society Ltd v Argyll Stores (Holdings) Ltd* (1998)). Contracts to build can, however, be specifically enforced provided that the construction contract sufficiently defines the work to be carried out, damages would be inadequate and the builder has already taken possession of the land on which the work is to be carried out: *Wolverhampton Corporation v Emmons* (1901);
- contracts involving personal services (e.g. an agreement by an actor to appear in a play): *Rigby v Connol* (1878). This exclusion is based upon

public policy grounds and the objection that enforcement would require continuous supervision;

- contracts to pay money because damages is clearly an adequate remedy: *South African Territories Ltd* (1898). In *Beswick v Beswick* (1968), however, the House of Lords departed from this traditional restriction and awarded specific performance of a contract whereby, in return for a transfer of a business, the transferee was to pay the transferor's widow the sum of £5 per week for life. Justice demanded an equitable remedy.

Defences to Specific Performance

Even though the contract may be of a type that is suitable for specific performance, the defendant may be able to invoke a defence to the claim. These include where:

- specific performance of only part of the contract is sought;
- there has been some misrepresentation or other default by the claimant (the "clean hands" maxim);
- the contract reflects a common mistake shared by the parties;
- there is some misdescription in the contract of the property to be transferred;
- there has been an unreasonable lapse of time ("laches") in seeking the order;
- it will cause hardship to the parties or to a third party. For example, in *Patel v Ali* (1984) specific performance of a land contract was denied in order to prevent "a hardship amounting to injustice". The plaintiff had to be content with damages;
- there is a want of mutuality, i.e. the remedy of specific performance is not available to the other party. For example, where one party is below the age of majority.

INJUNCTIONS

DEFINITION CHECKPOINT

An injunction may be granted against an individual, a class or an organisation restraining the unlawful acts of unidentified people. A person may seek an injunction to protect his existing private rights. Public rights are usually protected by injunctions obtained by the Attorney General. A local authority may also seek an injunction to protect public rights in the locality or to enforce planning control. To act in breach of an injunction is contempt of court.

Types of Injunction

Each type of injunction has been designed to achieve a different function. These categories include:

- **prohibitory injunctions** which forbid the party to do or to continue to do an unlawful act (e.g. to build upon land in breach of a restrictive covenant);
- **mandatory injunctions** which order that an act be undone (e.g. to demolish a building which has been built in breach of a restrictive covenant). Hence, a mandatory injunction when granted is likely to undo a wrongful act rather than to order the defendant to carry out a positive obligation. This is because of the difficulties of supervision: *Gravesham BC v British Railways Board* (1978). Mandatory injunctions are uncommon;
- **final injunctions** are granted in final settlement of the dispute between the parties and are issued at the completion of the court proceedings;
- **interim injunctions** (sometimes known as "interlocutory injunctions") which are made during the course of legal proceedings continue only until the eventual trial of the action. The purpose is to restrain the defendant immediately without waiting for a full court hearing;
- **without notice injunctions** are granted in an emergency without the other side having been informed or given the opportunity to attend the hearing of the application;
- **quia timet injunctions** which are designed to prevent an anticipatory infringement of the claimant's rights where an infringement is a realistic threat;
- **search orders** (formerly known as Anton Pillar orders) which authorise the claimant to enter the defendant's premises to inspect and seize documents relevant to the case. The aim is to protect evidence in relation to impending litigation;
- **freezing injunctions** (formerly known as Mareva injunctions) which prevent the defendant from taking his assets out of the jurisdiction of the court before the completion of litigation.

Guidelines for Interim Injunctions

A series of guidelines as to when interim injunctions should be granted were set out by Lord Diplock in *American Cyanamid Co v Ethicon Ltd* (1975). Subject to civil procedure rules these ensure that:

- the claimant's case must not be frivolous or vexatious and there must be a serious question to be tried. Previously the claimant had to show a strong prima facie case;
- a "balance of convenience" or "balance of justice" test must be satisfied. This test involves weighing up the potential harm suffered by the applicant

if no injunction is awarded, with the potential inconvenience caused to the defendant if it is granted. For example, in *Gregory v Castleoak Ltd* (2002) the loss to the claimant, if the injunction was not granted, was minimal whereas, if granted, it would be financially disastrous for the defendant. Importantly, the case for an injunction will be strengthened if the claimant is prepared to give an undertaking to the court to compensate the defendant for loss in the event of the eventual litigation being unsuccessful. If the claimant cannot afford to pay such potential damages, the court may refuse to order the injunction;

• only as a last resort will the strength of each party's case be considered. Nevertheless, in *Series 5 Software v Clarke* (1996) more emphasis was placed upon this last guideline. The claimant's case was weak and, in refusing to grant injunctive relief, Laddie J. adopted a more flexible approach. He was not prepared to relegate the strength of each party's case to the last resort.

Exceptions to Cyanamid

The *American Cyanamid* guidelines do not apply in the following situations:

• when there is no arguable defence. As a permanent injunction will be granted eventually, an interim injunction will be granted until the trial occurs;

• when the grant or refusal of an injunction will render the trial of the action unlikely. In *Cambridge Nutrition Ltd v BBC* (1990), the claimants unsuccessfully sought an injunction restraining the BBC from broadcasting a program until the publication of a government report. If the interim injunction had been granted, the claimants would have achieved their goal without a trial. The *Cyanamid* guidelines are inappropriate in such cases;

• when it is an interim *mandatory* injunction that is sought. It was demonstrated in *Shepherd Homes v Sandham* (1971) that the court will not usually require the defendant to take positive steps (e.g. the demolition of a building) before the issue has gone to trial;

• when it is a trade dispute (see s.221(2) of the Trade Union and Labour Relations (Consolidation) Act 1992);

• where a company seeks to restrain a creditor from presenting a winding-up petition;

• where s.12(3) of the Human Rights Act 1998 applies. This relates to the European Convention right to freedom of expression (art.10) and provides that no interim injunction is to be granted to restrain publication before trial unless the court is satisfied that the applicant is likely to be able to establish that the publication should not be allowed. This is a higher threshold than under the *Cyanamid* guidelines: *Cream Holdings v Banerjee* (2004).

Damages in Lieu of an Injunction

The general presumption is that, if a right is infringed, an injunction will be granted. In certain circumstances, however, the courts may award damages instead of injunctive relief. Following *Shelfer v City of London Electric Lighting Co Ltd* (1895), the working rule emerges that damages may be an alternative where:

* the claimant's loss is small;
* the loss can be valued in money terms;
* money would provide the claimant with adequate compensation; and
* an injunction would be oppressive, unduly harsh or disproportionate.

Illustrative cases

In *Tamares (Vincent Square) Ltd v Fairpoint Properties (Vincent Square) Ltd* (2006), Deputy Judge Moss refused to grant an injunction which would require part of a building to be knocked down because, "it would be 'oppressive' to grant a mandatory injunction which would create loss to the Defendants out of all conceivable proportion to any loss that might be suffered by the Claimant. The grant of a mandatory injunction would be unjust and inequitable and, in the exercise of my discretion, I am not prepared to grant it";

In *Daniells v Mendonca* (1999) the court granted a mandatory injunction for the removal of a building extension which involved a trespass on a neighbour's land. The reasoning here was that the claimant could not be adequately compensated by the small monetary payment that was likely to be awarded.

Search Order

This is an order preventing disposal by the defendant of any evidence prior to trial. It is especially important in commercial cases involving breach of confidence, copyright and passing off. The power to make a search order is now on a statutory footing: see s.7 of the Civil Procedure Act 1997. In *Anton Pillar KG v Manufacturing Processes Ltd* (1976), it was made clear that before an order will be made the following conditions must be met:

* there must be a strong prima facie case;
* the claimant must show actual or potential damage of a serious nature and
* there must be clear evidence that the defendant has incriminating documents or other items that are likely to be destroyed before the trial.

Safeguards

Guidelines on the execution of search orders were laid down in *Universal Thermosensors Ltd v Hibben* (1992). These include ensuring:

- the presence of a supervising solicitor (ideally with experience and not a member of the firm of solicitors acting for the claimant);
- the execution of the order in office hours;
- where the order pertains to a private house, perhaps occupied by a woman on her own, that the solicitor serving the order should be or should be accompanied by a woman;
- unless impracticable, that a list of items to be removed should be prepared at the premises and the defendant afforded an opportunity to check the list;
- that no items should be taken from the defendant's premises unless covered by the terms of the order;
- the setting aside of the order where the claimant or the claimant's solicitors have acted improperly;
- the availability of exemplary (i.e. punitive) damages for wrongful actions.

Freezing Injunctions

As in *Mareva Compania Naveira SA v International Bulkcarriers SA* (1975), these injunctions were originally granted where a claimant had brought an action in Britain against a foreign defendant who had assets within the jurisdiction that he might remove. It is now also possible to seek a freezing injunction where proceedings are started outside Britain. Freezing injunctions are now governed by s.37 of the **Supreme Court Act 1981** and the Civil Procedure Rules.

KEY CASE

THIRD CHANDRIS SHIPPING CORPORATION V UNIMARINE SA (1979)

In *Third Chandris Shipping Corporation v Unimarine SA* (1979), Lord Denning set out guidelines as to when a freezing injunction should be ordered. He suggested that the claimant should establish a good case by providing:

- a full and frank disclosure of all material matters;
- particulars of his claim against the defendant and the points made against it by the defendant;
- reasons for believing the defendant has assets within the jurisdiction;

- grounds for believing that the assets may be removed or dissipated before the claim is satisfied; and
- an undertaking that, if the litigation subsequently fails, the defendant will be compensated.

Worldwide freezing orders

A freezing order can still be made when the defendant's assets are located outside the jurisdiction of the court. Such an order, however, will be justified only in exceptional circumstances. In *BCCI SA (No.9)* (1994), a worldwide freezing order was made against certain employees of BCCI following a major international fraud. When such an order is made, the court will take an undertaking from the claimant that he will seek permission of the English court before attempting to enforce the order abroad. Such permission will be granted according to the following guidelines as set out in *Dadourian Group International Inc v Simms* (2006):

- the grant of permission should be "just and convenient" and "not oppressive to the parties";
- all relevant circumstances and options need to be considered. The onus is on the applicant to provide sufficient evidence to enable the judge to reach an informed decision;
- the court must balance the interests of all the parties;
- the applicant must show that there is a real prospect that the assets are located within the foreign jurisdiction;
- there must be evidence of a risk of dissipation of the assets in question;
- only in cases of urgency should the permission be given without the other party having notice of the application.

Revision Checklist

You should now know and understand:

- **the meaning of equity and its impact;**
- **the various maxims of equity;**
- **the remedy of specific performance and its availability;**
- **the types of injunction and their availability.**

QUESTION AND ANSWER

The Question

X, a local property developer, seeks your advice as to the availability of equitable remedies in light of the following claims against him:

(i) a claim by Y that X has breached a covenant to provide a night porter for the security and upkeep of the block of flats in which X resides;

(ii) a claim by X's neighbour Z, that X's building project will substantially limit the flow of light to Z's property. X has planned an extension to his home, which is in a state of partial construction.

Outlining what further information you require (if any), advise X as to the likely approach of the court and the principles upon which equitable relief will be granted or refused.

Advice and the Answer

This question requires a brief general outline of the jurisdiction of the court to award injunctions and grant orders for specific performance.

Part (i) involves a possible claim for an order for specific performance. In *Ryan v Mutual Tontine*, a landlord's covenant to employ a resident porter was not specifically enforced. The principal concern in such cases is the prospect of constant supervision by the courts, i.e. that the courts would be drawn into an indefinite series of rulings to ensure compliance with the order (*Co-Operative Insurance Society Ltd v Argyll*). The modern approach of the courts, however, is to consider the merit and practicality of enforcing each individual contract before them. As to Y's claim, more information is required and the courts would consider whether (a) there is sufficient definition of the obligations within the contract; (b) if enforcing compliance would involve supervision by the court to an unacceptable degree, and (c) the respective prejudices and hardships suffered by the parties if the order is made or not made. Accordingly, if the work of the porter is sufficiently defined, and involves no unacceptable degree of superintendence, then specific performance might be granted. Damages would not compensate for the loss of the feeling of security provided by a porter resident in the premises.

Part (ii) requires a discussion of the availability of injunctive relief both at an interim and final stage of proceedings. At trial, Z will need to prove the existence of his right to light and the extent to which the flow of light into his property has been diminished. At an interim stage, however, before the case is heard in full, Z may seek injunctive relief to restrain immediately the defendants continued building works.

The concern of the court at an interim stage is to minimise the risk of injustice to the parties given that the court has not yet had the opportunity to determine the case or to assess fully the strength of the parties' respective claims. If an interim injunction is granted, the claimant is required to enter into an undertaking that he will abide by any order as to damages which the court may make if it emerges that the claimant Z was not entitled to injunctive relief and X has suffered damage thereby. In determining the availability of interim relief in favour of Z, the *American Cyanamid* principles will be applied. At the heart of this approach, the balance of convenience is determined—that is, in short, the risk of injustice to the parties which would result from deciding the case in one way or in the other in the face of incomplete evidence. It is unlikely that Z would be awarded an interim mandatory order, i.e. to dismantle the building works to date. Although the court has jurisdiction to do so, the exercise of discretion is rare. As the case has not been heard in full, there is a very high risk of injustice to X, in that he will waste time, money and materials if wrongly mandated (*Shepherd Homes v Sandham*) and Z will receive all he seeks from the action, at an interim stage.

The principles governing final injunctions are general equitable principles, such as the adequacy of damages, the conduct of the parties, the possibility of hardship etc. If Z can show that his rights have been infringed an injunction may be granted to dismantle the offending works and prohibit infringement of Z's rights. The availability of damages in lieu of injunction may also be relevant. Under s.50 of the **Supreme Court Act 1981**, where the court has jurisdiction to award an injunction or to order specific performance, it may award damages in lieu. Further information is required as to the injury caused to Z. Under *Shelfer v City of London Electric Lighting Co*, AL Smith L.J. laid down the good working rule that damages may be awarded in lieu of injunction where, (a) the injury to the claimant is small; (b) the injury is one which is capable of being estimated in money; (c) the injury is one which can be adequately compensated by a small money payment, and (d) it would be oppressive to the defendant to grant an injunction. If nuisance caused by X can be demonstrated, the prima facie entitlement of Z is to an injunction.

The Trust

2

INTRODUCTION

This chapter examines the legal device known as the trust and distinguishes it from other types of legal relationships. The various types of trust are considered and particular emphasis is placed upon the distinction between express trusts and implied trusts.

Although trusts come in a variety of forms and cater for different types of property and purpose, they all share the same essential characteristics. At its heart, a trust involves the fragmentation of legal title (legal ownership) and equitable title (beneficial ownership). The legal title is vested in a character known as the "trustee" and the trustee holds the trust property on behalf of the "beneficiary". It is only on this separation of title that equitable ownership assumes importance because the general rule is that legal title carries with it all rights: *Westdeutsche Landesbank Girocentrale v London Islington BC* (1996).

The Fundamentals

The trustee owes a fiduciary duty (i.e. a duty of utmost good faith) to both the settlor and the beneficiary. The entitlement of the beneficiaries will normally be set out in the document creating the trust (the trust instrument), but where this is not the case the rights of the beneficiaries can be implied by equity. Trusts can be of any sort of property: land, money, chattels, cheques, debts, etc. Many trusts are nowadays created simply to maximise tax advantages.

Trusts Distinguished from Other Concepts

Bailment

This is a common law relationship which arises when goods owned by A are, with A's permission, in the possession of B. This may be a contractual relationship (e.g. if you leave your car in a secure airport car park while on holiday) or a gratuitous relationship (e.g. when you store furniture in a relative's attic). This is very different from a trust because there is no transfer of ownership involved and the duties expected of the bailee are much less extensive than those expected from a trustee.

Agency

This is the relationship between principal and agent and is normally contractual (e.g. you normally employ an agent, such as a solicitor or surveyor, to act on your behalf). The agent's job is to represent his principal's interests in dealings with third parties. An agent will not usually have title to the property vested in him, which means that, even if the agent has possession of goods, he will have no claim to ownership.

Contracts

These binding bilateral agreements differ from trusts in a variety of ways:

- a contract is a common law, personal obligation resulting from a negotiated agreement between the parties. A trust arises from equity and confers property rights on the beneficiary that can be enforced against both the property itself and third parties;
- a contract is valid only if supported by consideration or made by deed. A beneficiary under a properly constituted trust, however, can enforce the trust even though he has not given any consideration;
- a contract cannot usually be enforced by third parties ("privity of contract" is necessary). This rule is, however, subject to certain statutory exceptions contained, for example, in the **Contracts (Rights of Third Parties) Act 1999** and s.56 of the Law of Property Act 1925. In contrast, a beneficiary can always enforce a trust, even if he is not a party to the agreement that created the trust.

Debts

These are usually contractual (e.g. when I agree to repay a loan to my bank). A debt is a personal obligation whereas the interest of a beneficiary under a trust is a proprietary right. This distinction becomes clear on the insolvency of the person in whom the property is vested. If a trust is in existence, the trust property will not be available to the trustee's creditors. Where there is no trust, any creditor will be able to claim against the bankrupt's estate.

KEY CASES

BARCLAYS BANK LTD V QUISTCLOSE INVESTMENTS LTD (1970) AND RE KAYFORD LTD (1975)

- *Barclays Bank Ltd v Quistclose Investments Ltd* (1970) Here Rolls Razor Ltd declared a dividend on shares which it could not pay. Quistclose agreed to make a loan specifically for the purpose of paying the dividends. The money was paid into a special account at Barclays Bank.

Rolls then went into liquidation, leaving a large overdraft at Barclays. The Bank laid claim to the money in the special account in order to discharge the overdraft. The House of Lords held that, as Quistclose had paid the money for a particular purpose, on the failure of that purpose the Bank held the money on an implied trust for Quistclose. This is an example of an implied "resulting trust". The Bank was not, therefore, entitled to the money. The fact that there was a contract for a loan from Quistclose did not exclude the implication of a trust.

- *Re Kayford Ltd* (1975) Here a mail order company opened a special "Customers' Trust Deposit Account" at its bank for advance payments received from its customers. This money was not available to its liquidator when the company was subsequently wound up. By opening the account, the company demonstrated the intention to create a trust of the prepayments in favour of its customers. The obligations were transferred from debt to trust. The money was not, therefore, available to its general creditors. This is viewed as an express trust.

Gifts

These involve the absolute and gratuitous transfer of title to the property to be donated. For example, if I hand you £20 for your birthday, once the money is physically passed between us, I cannot later insist that you pay it back. The money is unconditionally yours. If, instead, I hand you £20 and tell you to give it to X when you next see him, then very different considerations apply. I (the settlor) have created a trust whereby you (the trustee) hold the money on trust for X (the beneficiary). It is not yours to keep and, if you spend it, you can be personally liable to account for its loss.

Dispositive powers of appointment

Powers are discretionary and permissive whereas a trust is imperative and mandatory. These powers must always operate behind a trust and they allow the donee the discretion to divert trust money from the beneficiaries in favour of another person or purpose, but only to the extent as permitted by the settlor. An example of a power of appointment is where a trust is set up and the trustee is given the power to donate up to £500 to charity. If this power was not given, any donation would be unauthorised and in breach of trust. This power, therefore, allows the trustee lawfully to siphon some of the trust fund away from the beneficiaries. It is, however, purely up to the trustee to decide whether or not to give any money to charity. The trustee must, however, address his mind to whether or not to exercise the power. The distinction between a power and a trust is important, but is not always easy to draw.

Distinguishing powers from trusts

- a power can be legal (as with a power of attorney) or equitable. Trusts are always equitable;
- a power is discretionary whereas a trust imposes a duty. Accordingly, if a trustee does not carry out his duties the court will intervene and compel him to do so. The court will not intervene to compel a person to exercise a power;
- unlike the beneficiary under a trust, a potential beneficiary under a power has no interest in the property before the power is exercised;
- the rule of certainty of objects (considered in Chapter 3) was once different for powers than for trusts. Prior to *McPhail v Doulton* (1971), all trustees would need a full list of potential beneficiaries before they could carry out their duties. This was unnecessary where someone had only a power. It was sufficient if it could be said of any given individual that he or she was or was not within the class of objects specified by the donor of the power. The rule for powers has now been extended to discretionary trusts. The old complete list rule still applies to fixed trusts.

CLASSIFICATION OF TRUSTS

Figure 2: Types of Trust

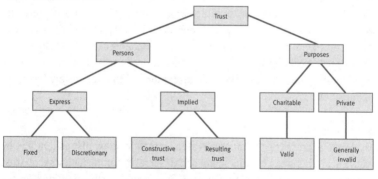

Express trusts

> **DEFINITION CHECKPOINT**
>
> These Trusts are intentionally created either by the settlor expressly declaring himself to be a trustee or by transferring the property to a third party trustee to hold on stipulated trusts. As a general rule, express trusts may be created by deed, will, writing or orally. The overwhelming majority of trusts are created in this way. There are several brands of express trust.

Private trusts

A private trust is a trust for the benefit of either a named individual (e.g. "£50,000 to be held on trust for John") or a named class of individuals (e.g. "£50,000 to be held on trust for my children"). Private trusts can be fixed or discretionary in nature. They cannot, however, be used to advance a purpose as there would be no one to enforce the trust. Subject to some odd exceptions, there is no such thing as a private purpose trust. Hence, a trust to promote duck shooting (not being charitable) will fail.

Public trusts

A public trust is a trust that is to benefit charity. This can be to benefit a named charitable organisation or to promote a charitable purpose (e.g. "£50,000 to relieve poverty in Africa"). Public purpose trusts are enforceable by the Attorney General and the Charity Commission.

Fixed trusts

A fixed trust is in contrast to a discretionary trust (below) and is a trust where the beneficiaries and their shares are fixed (i.e. stipulated) by the settlor, e.g. "£50,000 to be divided equally between Jack and Jill".

Discretionary trusts

A discretionary trust takes its name from the fact that the settlor gives the trustee the discretion to select who, from a given class of persons, will receive the trust property and, normally, in what shares. For example, "£50,000 to be divided between such of my children as my trustee shall nominate". No beneficiary under a discretionary trust has any property rights until the trustee exercises his discretion. All the beneficiary has is an expectation.

Secret trusts

These are express trusts that are created by testamentary disposition (i.e. by will). Secret trusts can be fully secret or half secret in nature. A fully secret trust arises where, on the face of the will, X appears to leave an unconditional legacy to Y, but Y had previously agreed with X to hold the property on trust for Z. Note that the will makes no reference whatsoever to the existence of the trust. A half secret trust arises where the will makes express reference to the existence of a trust, but does not disclose the terms of that trust. An example would be where by will X bequeaths "£100,000 to Y on trusts that I have previously communicated to Y".

Pension Trusts

Private pension trusts (otherwise known as "superannuation schemes") are popular and attractive. In order to maximise fiscal advantages, the scheme must be approved by the Pensions Regulator and the HM Revenue & Customs. Under such schemes, the employee makes financial contributions through the "pay as you earn" scheme administered by the employer. The employee receives income tax relief as regards these pay as you earn payments. The employer will also make contributions to the pension scheme. The trustees will invest the entire pension fund and, on the retirement of an employee, the idea is that there should be sufficient funds to provide a taxable pension for the retirement years. The payment may be calculated as a percentage of the employee's final salary ("final salary schemes") or may reflect the money earned as a result of the individual's total contributions to the fund ("money purchase schemes"). The use of a trust operates to separate the pension funds from the employer's funds and to maximise tax advantages. The Pensions Acts of 1995 and 2004 aim to protect beneficiaries from the effects of poor administration, fraud and employer's insolvency. The schemes are policed by the Pensions Regulator and the Pensions Ombudsman may investigate complaints of maladministration of the fund. A Pension Protection Fund exists to provide limited compensation for those who suffer loss by reason of a pension fund being in deficit.

Protective trusts

A protective trust is aimed at ensuring that a feckless beneficiary will not lose the trust property to his creditors or sell his trust interest to someone else. The way in which this protection is achieved is by giving the beneficiary a life interest in the property which is made determinable (i.e. is to be forfeited) on a given event (e.g. bankruptcy or assignment). From the ashes of the life interest emerges a discretionary trust in favour of specified beneficiaries. Hence there are two trusts. Following s.33 of the Trustee Act 1925, the process of creating a protective trust has been greatly simplified. It was once necessary to set out the terms of the protective trust in detail. Since 1925, however, all the settlement must now do is contain reference to the intention to create a protective trust. The terms of that trust are then implied by s.33. This section provides that the income will be held upon trust for the principal beneficiary until his protected life interest is forfeited. On the failure of this life interest, the income is to be held upon discretionary trust for the benefit of:

- the principal beneficiary, his spouse and children, or
- if there is no spouse or children, the principal beneficiary and the persons who would, if he were actually dead, be entitled to the trust property.

Implied Trusts

> ### ▌DEFINITION CHECKPOINT
>
> These are trusts which are not expressly created and which arise by implication or by operation of law. They include resulting trusts, constructive trusts and trusts imposed by statute. The boundaries between resulting trusts and constructive trusts are not, however, always clear.

Resulting trusts

The resulting trust takes its name from the fact that it operates to ensure that beneficial title "results back" to a transferor (see Chapter 9). This is more easily understood by considering the circumstances in which the resulting trust may arise.

- Where one party transfers legal title to property to another in return for no consideration, a presumption of a resulting trust is raised. This is sometimes called a "voluntary conveyance resulting trust". The equitable interest will result back to the transferor.
- Where property is purchased by X with some financial assistance from Y then Y may acquire an interest in the property by virtue of a purchase money resulting trust. Such a trust will be relevant only when there is no common intention to share the property beneficially and when the payments were made to the acquisition cost of the property. The examples so far concern what is traditionally called the "presumed intention resulting trust".
- When a settlor who intends to create an express trust fails in some way to dispose of the entire equitable interest then that which remains results back to the settlor. This third class is sometimes called an "automatic resulting trust" because it is traditionally perceived to be an automatic response to the failure to deal with the property fully and effectively. The modern view, however, is that it is merely a species of the "presumed intention resulting trust".

> ### DEFINITION CHECKPOINT
>
> The constructive trust is very different to the resulting trust (see
> Chapter 10). It is a trust imposed to ensure good conscience and,
> originally, had nothing to do with the intention of the parties. A
> constructive trust is traditionally invoked in a variety of situations, for
> example, in relation to mutual wills, fully secret trusts, unauthorised
> profits made by a trustee and the doctrine of conversion on a specifically
> enforceable contract. The constructive trust now has a very different
> sphere in which to operate and this is in relation to the joint purchase of
> the family home. Indeed, the constructive trust has largely subsumed
> the relevance of the resulting trust in this area of the law.

The family home

There are two scenarios where this family home constructive trust will arise:

*   when there has been some discussion, arrangement or understanding
    between the parties as to beneficial ownership of the property. If a non-
    owning party acts to his detriment on the strength of that understanding,
    an express bargain constructive trust will arise and the court will give
    effect to the bargain reached;
*   when the parties have no discussion at all about the fate of the beneficial
    ownership of the property, but the non-owner makes direct financial
    contributions to the purchase of the property, there will be an implied
    bargain constructive trust. This type of trust arises from the presumed
    common intentions of the parties as evidenced by the course of dealings
    between them.

Statutory Trusts

> ### DEFINITION CHECKPOINT
>
> Statutory trusts are imposed in certain specific circumstances. The major
> example is where there are joint legal owners of land. By virtue of the
> Trusts of Land and Appointment of Trustees Act 1996, the joint owners
> must necessarily hold the legal title on statutory trust for themselves
> and/or others. Statutory trusts arise also on bankruptcy, intestacy and
> on the conveyance of land to minor.

Revision Checklist

You should now know and understand:

- the structure and mechanics of the trust;
- how to distinguish a trust from other legal relationships;
- the distinction between fixed and discretionary trusts;
- the distinction between express and implied trusts.

QUESTION AND ANSWER

The Question

With reference to the following, explain the nature and operation of a trust:

a) the connection between the trust and Equity;
b) the separation of legal and equitable ownership and its practical implications;
c) the distinction between fixed trusts and discretionary trusts and the implications for the beneficiary.

Advice and the Answer

The question requires an account of the origins of the trust and its development and refinement by the conscience based jurisdiction known as Equity. This would include:

- a narrative concerning the separation of law and equity;
- a consideration of the practical distinction between the trustee's role as legal owner (i.e. the management and control of the trust property) and the beneficiary's role as equitable owner (i.e. entitlement to benefit of the trust property);
- the nature of fixed and discretionary trusts and trustee's distributive functions under each;
- the differences between the two types of trust with emphasis upon the basic obligations and rights under both types of trust;
- the added problems of enforcement experienced by a beneficiary under a discretionary trust.

The Three Certainties

....

3

INTRODUCTION

This chapter is concerned with the core ingredients of a valid trust which are often described as the three certainties. Each certainty will be examined in turn and the various principles, distinctions and requirements of each identified.

Due to the onerous duties placed upon a trustee, it is necessary that the settlor makes clear that a trust was intended, what property is subject to the trust and who the beneficiaries are in order that the trust can be enforced. Accordingly, the law has developed a test known as the "three certainties" that encompasses certainty of intention, certainty of subject matter and certainty of objects (Lord Langdale M.R. in *Knight v Knight* (1840)). Except as to charitable trusts which do not need certainty of objects (see below), the three certainties need to be present so that a trust can be workable and capable of supervision by the court.

....

CERTAINTY OF INTENTION

It is necessary for the settlor to intend to create a trust as opposed to some other type of legal relationship. Nevertheless, there is no magic formula necessary to show the intention to create a trust. Equity looks to the intent rather than to the form. Although desirable, the use of the word "trust" is not essential. Even if the term "trust" is employed, this is no guarantee that a trust will be discerned: *Midland Bank v Wyatt* (1995). There is no general requirement that a trust be created or even evidenced in writing and a trust can even be inferred from the conduct of the parties and the surrounding circumstances.

Precatory Words
Precatory words are words merely of hope and desire, e.g. "in the hope that", "I would like that", "I desire that" and "I feel confident that". Although in the older cases precatory words were sometimes sufficient to create a trust, since the late nineteenth century this is no longer the case. The court is now looking for imperative words that impose a mandatory obligation on the trustee. A moral obligation is not enough: *Sweeney v Coghill* (1998). If there is doubt, the burden lies on the claimant to establish the necessary intention on a balance of probabilities: *Re Snowden* (1979).

Lambe v Eames (1871), Re Adams and the Kengsington Vestry (1884) and Margulies v Margulies (1999)

- In *Lambe v Eames* (1871), the testator gave his estate to his widow "to be at her disposal in any way she thinks best for the benefit of herself and her family". It was held that these were precatory words and did not create a trust.
- In *Re Adams and the Kensington Vestry* (1884), the gift was made "in full confidence that she will do what is right as to the disposal thereof between my children either in her lifetime or by will after her decease". These precatory words ensured that no trust was created.
- In *Margulies v Margulies* (1999), a legacy of a residuary estate was left to one son and expressed to be in confidence that, "if in the interests of family harmony", he would make provision for his brother and sister. As the words used were precatory in nature, the son could keep the money for himself.

Anomalous cases

There are two decisions that, at first glance, seem to contradict the modern rule that precatory words will not create a trust.

- *Comiskey v Bowring-Hanbury* (1905) where the House of Lords held that in looking for certainty of words or intention one should construe the document as a whole. There a testamentary gift to the widow "in full confidence" that she leave the property on her death to one or more of his nieces, did not prevent the creation of a trust in favour of the nieces. This was because the settlor went on to make what is called a gift over in default of appointment. The added words that proved crucial were, "in default of any disposition by her . . . I hereby direct that all my estate and property acquired by her under my will shall at her death be equally divided among my nieces". The imperative wording of the gift over imposed the mandatory obligation on the widow. She held the property on trust for herself for life and then in remainder for the nieces equally. This case should not, therefore, be cited as authority for saying that precatory words can constitute a trust;
- *Re Steele's Will Trusts* (1948) where a solicitor drafted a trust for his client that followed an outmoded precedent which featured precatory

words. Although this may have worked in the past to create a trust, it should have failed for a lack of certainty of intention. Nevertheless, the court concluded that the deliberate use of the precedent (albeit itself defective) demonstrated the necessary intention. This is a maverick case that turns upon its own facts and is of dubious authority.

Inferred Intentions
Even though there may be no express verbal recognition that a trust was intended, the requisite intention might still be inferred by the court. This inference may arise equally in both a family and a commercial context and it is convenient to consider each stream of case law separately.

Family context
In *Paul v Constance* (1977) the intention to create a trust was identified as Mr Constance had repeatedly said to Ms Paul about his bank account, "The money is as much yours as mine". This was not a gift, but was instead a declaration of a trust that gave Ms Paul an equal share in the bank account. Similarly, in *Gold v Hill* (1999), Mr Gilbert took out a life assurance policy. The named beneficiary of the policy was Mr Gold. Mr Gilbert had, however, said to Mr Gold that he wanted the insurance money to be used to look after his mistress, Carol, and her children. This conversation had the effect of nominating Mr Gold as a trustee.

A gift is not a trust
There must, however, be the intention to declare a trust and not the intention to make an immediate gift. In *Jones v Lock* (1865) a father held out a cheque, which was payable to him, in front of his child and said "I give this to baby". This was a failed gift (the title to the cheque did not pass) and could not be construed as a declaration of trust.

Commercial context
In this context, a trust is inferred usually as a guard against the possibility of the recipient of funds becoming insolvent. For example, a solicitor will pay money received on behalf of clients into a specially designated "client account" and, by doing so, that account will be shielded from the claims of the solicitor's other creditors. Similarly, a lender may advance money to the recipient on condition that the money be used only for a specified purpose with the result that property rights in those funds do not move from the lender unless and until the money is deployed for that specified purpose.

BARCLAYS BANK V QUISTCLOSE (1970), TWINSECTRA V YARDLEY (2002) AND RE KAYFORD (1975)

- *Barclays Bank v Quistclose* (1970) concerned an implied trust created by the payment of money to Rolls Razor Ltd (borrowed specifically from Quistclose to pay dividends to shareholders) into a separate bank account held at Barclays Bank. The mutual intentions (of the payer and the recipient) had been that the money was to be held on trust unless it was employed for the purpose specified. Note that if the purpose had been achieved, Quistclose would have been treated like any other unsecured creditor of the company;
- *Twinsectra v Yardley* (2002) involved a solicitor receiving money from a lender (Twinsectra) on behalf of a client (Yardley). The solicitor gave an undertaking that the money would be retained by them and used only for the purposes of purchasing property for the client. The solicitor, however, used the money for other purposes and did not repay the loan. The limitations placed upon the use of the funds advanced demonstrated the existence of a trust. Under this trust the solicitor held the money for the benefit of Twinsectra, subject to the power of the solicitor to use it for the purposes specified;
- *Re Kayford* (1975) concerned advance payments made by customers for goods which were placed into a "Customers' Trust Deposit Account". The company became insolvent and the general creditors laid claim to the money. The steps taken by the company overtly demonstrated its intention to create a trust. Here the necessary intention was inferred from the unilateral conduct of the company.

Absence of Intention

There are two possible variations. First, if the property is transferred to a third party, and there is no intention to create a trust, the transfer will amount to an absolute gift to the donee: *Lassence v Tierney* (1848). Secondly, where the settlor unsuccessfully declares himself to be a trustee no title passes and the property remains in the settlor's estate.

CERTAINTY OF SUBJECT MATTER

Although any existing property may be the subject matter of a trust, it is necessary that the settlor identify what is to be the subject of the trust and provide the means by which the interests of the beneficiaries can be ascertained. If not, the trust must fail for lack of certainty and cannot be enforced.

Trust Property Must be Certain

The entire property that is to be the subject of the trust must be described in such a way that it becomes certain and ascertainable. There has to be an identifiable trust fund. For example, in *Hemmens v Wilson Browne* (1995) a document purported to give X the right to a monetary payment of £110,000 at any time from Y. This did not create a trust because there was no fund identified from which the money was to be paid. In *Palmer v Simmonds* (1854) a declaration concerning the "bulk of my said residuary estate" was held to be ineffective to create a trust. "Bulk" has no clear meaning and is totally uncertain.

Tangibles and intangibles

A distinction is to be drawn between trusts of tangibles (i.e. something which has physical form) and intangibles (something without physical form such as shares, money and debts). The major difference is that with tangibles the physical segregation of the trust property from other property is necessary. Conversely, with intangibles no segregation is required.

KEY CASES

RE GOLDCORP EXCHANGE LTD (1995) AND HUNTER V MOSS (1994)

- *Re Goldcorp Exchange Ltd* (1995). This case concerned a dealer in precious metals who became insolvent. A number of customers sought the delivery of gold (a tangible) that they had recently purchased. Unfortunately, the gold was unallocated and could not be individually identified. There could be no trust because the subject matter was not ascertainable.
- *Hunter v Moss* (1994). This involved Mr Hunter who was entitled, under his contract of employment with Mr Moss, to claim 50 shares (intangibles) out of 950 shares in a particular company held by his employer. Although it was not possible to identify precisely which 50 shares were intended to be the subject matter of the trust, the trust was upheld. Since the shares were essentially identical and indistinguishable, any 50 shares in the company were capable of forming the subject matter of the trust.

A trust of the residue of an estate

A residuary estate may form the subject matter of a trust. For example, if a testator leaves a will containing a number of legacies and creates a trust of "whatever is left", there is certainty of subject matter. The executors can readily calculate the residual estate. There are cases, however, which might be thought to conflict and, turning on the presence or not of a life interest, are apt to cause difficulties.

KEY CASES

ESTATE OF LAST (1958), SPRANGE V BARNARD (1789), AND
RE JONES (1898)

- In the *Estate of Last* (1958), property was left to a brother on terms that "at his death anything that is left, that came from me" was to pass to specified persons. This was held to be a trust because the brother only had a life interest in the property. A similar approach was adopted in *Re Thompson* (1879) where the subject matter of the trust was identified as "anything remaining" on a wife's death. This was upheld as a trust because the widow only had a life interest in her deceased husband's estate.
- In *Sprange v Barnard* (1789), however, a wife left stock to her husband for his own use on terms that "the remaining part of what is left that he does not want for his own wants" should be bequeathed to specified individuals. The trust failed because at its creation there was a total uncertainty of subject matter.
- In *Re Jones* (1898), a trust of "such parts of my . . . estate as she shall not have sold" failed for uncertainty of subject matter. The legatee was given an absolute interest in the property and, therefore, it could be entirely dissipated. Where, however, a life interest in the property is given, the capital cannot be touched and, therefore, the subject matter of the trust is known at the outset.

Beneficial Interest Must be Certain

Not only must the trust property be certain and ascertainable, but (except as regards discretionary trusts where the beneficial interests are never certain) each beneficiary's share under the trust must also be allocated in some way when the trust is established: *Curtis v Rippon* (1820).

Boyce v Boyce (1849) and Re Golay (1965)

- In *Boyce v Boyce* (1849) a fixed trust was set up by will on the death of the testator. The trust property consisted of two houses and there were two named beneficiaries, Maria and Charlotte. Maria was to choose which house she wanted. The other house was to be held on trust for Charlotte. Maria predeceased the testator and died without making any selection. As it was now impossible to say which house Charlotte should have, the entire trust had to fail for uncertainty of beneficial share. Both properties, therefore, stayed in the settlor's estate. The difficulty here was that the testator had prescribed a method of allocation that had subsequently become impossible.

- In *Re Golay* (1965) a trust was established to provide to Tossy "a reasonable income from my other properties". Tossy's beneficial interest was held to be certain because the use of the word "reasonable" provided an objective yardstick that the court could employ to calculate what a reasonable income for her would be. This provided the court with a method of ascertaining her beneficial interest. The court could look to her standard of living, income, needs, outgoings, etc. and conjure up an appropriate sum of money. This benevolent approach could not apply if the trust was of, say, "a reasonable legacy", "reasonable share", "reasonable amount" or "reasonable sum". The logic is that a reasonable income for an individual will be the same regardless of how much money is in the trust fund. It is capable of independent, objective assessment. Conversely, a reasonable share is subjective in that it may vary according to how much money is left. For example, if I use your lottery numbers and promise to give you a reasonable share of any eventual winnings then what is reasonable will vary wildly according to whether I win £10 or £10 million.

Equity is equality

As regards fixed trusts, the equitable maxim equity is equality might be brought into play to save an otherwise invalid trust. This was demonstrated in *Burrough v Philcox* (1840) where a trust was set up to benefit the settlor's son and daughter. Their shares, however, were not specified. By relying upon the maxim, each was deemed to have an equal share. The maxim can be invoked only where there is no contrary intention shown. If the trust is "to benefit my children unequally", the maxim could not apply and the trust would necessarily fail.

Uncertain subject matter?
Where there is no certainty of trust property, there can be no trust. The property, whatever it is, will remain with the settlor or if he is dead will either pass by will or under the intestacy rules. If, however, the trust fails for uncertainty of beneficial share then, if the trust property has already been transferred to the trustee, it will be held on resulting trust for the settlor. If legal title has not moved, then the property remains with the settlor.

CERTAINTY OF OBJECTS

There have to be beneficiaries (i.e. objects of the trust) who are certain or capable of being rendered certain: *Re Endacott* (1950). This is because there has to be someone who can enforce the trust. This rule does not, however, apply to charitable trusts because the Attorney General and Charity Commission can enforce such public trusts. As will become clear, a private trust can fail for conceptual uncertainty, evidential uncertainty, administrative unworkability and/or capriciousness.

Fixed Trusts
In relation to fixed trusts (i.e. where the interests of the beneficiaries are specified in the trust instrument), the courts take a strict approach. The trust is void unless each and every beneficiary is ascertainable: *Morice v Bishop of Durham* (1804). This is called the complete list test. A trust will not fail, however, because a particular beneficiary cannot be found or there are doubts as to whether the beneficiary is still alive. In such cases, the money can be paid into court and steps then taken either to trace or to confirm the existence of the beneficiary. If the trustee decides eventually to distribute the trust property amongst the known beneficiaries, this will be done on the basis that any new claimant can recover against them: *Re Benjamin* (1902).

Discretionary Trusts
A discretionary trust arises where the trustee is given the discretion to select who, amongst a specified class of beneficiaries, will benefit under the trust. In modern times, the discretionary trust is used to benefit large groups of people such as employees and dependants. In such cases, a complete list might be a practical impossibility.

The class test
Since *McPhail v Doulton* (1971), the rule for certainty of objects for discretionary trusts is the same as for powers of appointment. The test is whether it can be

said with certainty of any potential claimant that he is or is not a member of the class. This is known as the class test and is less strict than the complete list test. The problem with the class test is how it is to be applied. The potential difficulty lies with proving a negative: how can a trustee prove that a particular person is not, for example, a relative of the deceased? This issue was subsequently addressed in *Re Baden (No.2)* (1973). This case concerned a trust to benefit "relatives" and "dependants". Although the trust was upheld, the Court of Appeal did not speak with one voice concerning the operation of the class test.

The views of the Court of Appeal

* Megaw L.J. saw the class test as being satisfied where, as regards a substantial number of beneficiaries, it can be said that they fall within the scope of the trust. This would be so even where there are others about whom it cannot be said with certainty that they are inside or outside the class. Accordingly, it did not matter that there were some "don't knows". This is so even though the trustee is making a selection from a narrower class than that intended by the settlor;
* Stamp L.J. took the literal approach that the class test could be satisfied only if it could be said of every potential claimant that they were or were not within the class. There is no room for any doubt with this approach. This signals a retreat to the previously jettisoned complete list test;
* Sachs L.J. felt that the class test was that, if a potential claimant could not prove that he was within the class, he was presumed to be outside the class. Hence, there is no room for a "don't know" category. Although superficially attractive, this approach allows for the fact that there might be numerous individuals who cannot prove their entitlement. It also caters for the possibility of a discretionary trust being upheld in circumstances where only one beneficiary can prove positively that he is in the class. This is clearly not what the settlor would ever have intended.

Conceptual and Evidential Uncertainty

> **DEFINITION CHECKPOINT**
>
> The description of the beneficiaries must, as regards both fixed and discretionary trusts, be conceptually certain.

* *Conceptual certainty* refers to semantic or linguistic expression (i.e. precision of language) as regards the class that is to benefit. For example, in

Re Barlow (1970) a trust to benefit "old friends" was conceptually uncertain. The terms "old" and "friend" have so many shades of meaning that it was impossible to say who was intended to benefit. As mentioned, in *Re Baden (No.2)*, the terms "relatives" and "dependants" were held to be conceptually certainty.

- **Evidential uncertainty** is thought only to apply to fixed trusts (see Sachs L.J. in *Re Baden (No.2)*). Such uncertainty arises where there is an absence of evidence to show who was intended to benefit under the trust. For example, a fixed trust to benefit such students of Nutshell University who graduated in 1990 with a first class degree in law. If the records of Nutshell University have been destroyed by fire then it will be impossible to draw up a complete list of beneficiaries and, therefore, the trust will fail for evidential uncertainty.

Width of Class and Administrative Unworkability

This is to do with the numbers of potential beneficiaries. In *McPhail v Doulton* (1971), Lord Wilberforce admitted that a class of beneficiaries might be so wide as not to constitute a class at all and this would make the trust (whether fixed or discretionary) administratively workable. By way of illustration, he suggested that a trust for "all the residents of Greater London" would be void. Hence, in *Re Hay's Settlement* (1982), it was accepted that a trust to benefit anyone in the world would be ineffective. In *R. v District Auditor Ex p. West Yorkshire Metropolitan CC* (1986), an attempt to benefit "any or all the inhabitants in the County of West Yorkshire" failed because the class (approximately 2.5 million people) was too large.

Capriciousness

A trust can be void if it is capricious, i.e. it reflects a nonsensical intention on the part of the settlor and precludes any sensible consideration by the trustees. For example, a trust to benefit red haired women would be struck down as capricious. In *Re Manisty's Settlement* (1974), Templeman J. provided the example of an attempt to benefit the residents of Greater London as being capricious. In *R. v District Auditor Ex p. West Yorkshire Metropolitan CC*, however, the court held that the trust which purported to benefit 2.5 million inhabitants was not capricious. There have been no cases decided on the basis capriciousness.

No Certainty of Objects?

Where there is an absence of certainty of objects, two possible consequences may arise.

- If the settlor is himself the trustee then nothing at all happens. No property has left the estate of the settlor.
- If however, a third party has been appointed as trustee then, on failure of the trust, the property will be held upon resulting trust for the settlor (or his estate).

Figure 3: Summary of rules on certainties

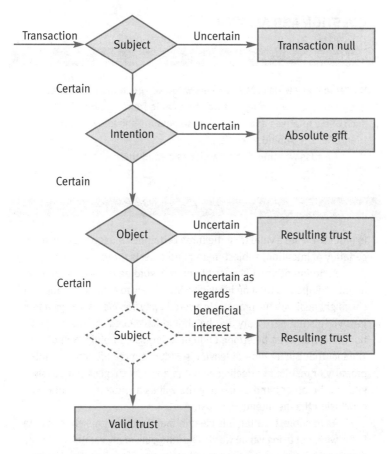

Revision Checklist

You should now know and understand:

- **the need for the certainties;**
- **the requirements of each certainty;**

- the different rules and distinctions which apply as regards each head of certainty;

- the case law which illustrates what is necessary to be established before a trust can be said to exist.

QUESTION AND ANSWER

The Question

Buster leaves all his property to his wife "secure in the knowledge that upon her death anything she has that came from me she will leave to such of my relatives and such of those persons she knows to be my old friends as she should think fit".

Discuss whether this establishes a valid trust.

Advice and the Answer

In order to create a valid trust the three certainties must be established; certainty of intention, subject-matter and objects (*Knight v Knight*).

As to intention, it is possible on the wording that Buster did not intend to impose a trust on his widow but merely to express a hope that she might deal with the property in a certain way (*Re Adams & Kensington Vestry*). It is not necessary that he should have used the word "trust", but the words must be strong enough to impose an obligation on her. The fact that Buster did not leave his widow a mere life interest in the property or restrict her dealing with it in any way suggests an absolute gift. On the other hand construing the will as a whole may lead to the conclusion that he intended a trust.

As to subject matter, it is clear in that Buster left his entire estate to his wife, not using vague words like "the bulk of my estate" (*Palmer v Simmonds*). However, it is not clear what the size of her beneficial interest is. It may be that the wife should have only a life interest (*Re Last*). In such a case, although entitled to the income, she would not be entitled to the capital. In *Sprange v Barnard* where a testatrix left her property to her husband Sprange for his sole use and "at his death the remaining part of what is left, that he does not want for his own wants and uses" to be left to others, the court held Sprange was absolutely entitled to the property on the ground that the property was uncertain.

As to objects, the trust for friends and relatives is a discretionary trust so there is no need for a complete list of beneficiaries (*McPhail v Doulton*). It must however be possible to say of any given person that he is or is not a relative or friend. Taking relatives to mean next of kin (per Stamp L.J. in *Re Baden (No.2)*), the class is conceptually certain but an old friend is too vague: *Re Barlow's Will Trusts*. This would mean that the class would be conceptually uncertain were it not for the provision that the widow is to decide who the testator's old friends are. It is permissible for a third party to determine who should be within the class (*Re Tuck Settlement Trusts*: questions of Jewish blood and faith should be determined by the Chief Rabbi). Taking the whole clause together it appears that the testator did not wish to restrict his widow's use of the property during her life and was happy to rely on her judgment for its disposal on her death. The tenor of the clause is not to create a trust, but to give her an absolute gift on the assumption that she would want on her death to leave the property to his friends and relatives.

Constitution of Trusts

4

INTRODUCTION

This Chapter focuses upon the circumstances in which a trust may be properly constituted or, put more simply, it considers the circumstances where a trustee will have sufficient title to the property in order for the trust to be effective. If the trust is not properly constituted, equity cannot usually offer assistance because of two interrelated and venerated maxims "equity will not assist a volunteer" and "equity will not perfect an imperfect gift": see *Jones v Lock* (1865). Constitution can occur by means of an effective self-declaration of trust or an effective transfer of property to the trustees: *Milroy v Lord* (1862).

SELF-DECLARATION AS TRUSTEE

A settlor with a legal interest in property can declare himself a trustee of that property for a beneficiary. This is the less popular method of creating a trust because, somewhat obviously, it can only be created during the lifetime of the settlor (i.e. it only relates to inter vivos trusts). It will also mean that the onerous, and usually unwelcome, duties of a trustee will rest with the person who has just divested himself of beneficial ownership over the property.

Key Points
- the general rule is that such declaration can be oral without the need for any additional formality. An exception applies in the case of land when the trust must be evidenced in writing and signed by the settlor but not his agent: s.53(1)(b) of the **Law of Property Act 1925**;
- the settlor can use any form of words to demonstrate the intention to create a trust. Intention can also be inferred from conduct;
- it is crucial to bear in mind that an ineffective gift cannot be construed as a declaration of trust. This is because the settlor has shown the intention to give the property away absolutely and has evinced no intention to retain the legal estate on trust for the intended donee: *Jones v Lock* (1865).

TRANSFER TO TRUSTEES

Types of Property

The settlor must transfer the title to the property to the trustee in the proper form. As will become clear, the mode of transfer varies with the nature of the property concerned.

- **Land.** Subject to exceptions relating to short leases, s.52 of the **Law of Property Act 1925** requires a deed of conveyance to transfer legal title to land. In the case of registered land, the transfer only becomes complete on its registration at the Land Registry.
- **Shares.** Legal title to shares is transferred traditionally by executing what is called a share transfer form followed by registration of the new owner in the company's shareholding register. It is upon registration that the transfer is complete. As regards a public company, registration will automatically follow on from the documentary transfer. A private company, however, usually has the discretion to refuse to register a share transfer dealing.
- **Chattels.** Title to chattels is transferred either by deed of gift (uncommon) or by physical delivery of the item to the recipient coupled with the intention to effect a transfer. Delivery includes parting with dominion over an article (e.g. passing over the key to a jewellery box).
- **Cheques.** Legal title to a cheque passes on endorsement by the transferor and delivery of the cheque to the third party. This, seemingly, is not possible when the cheque is crossed "account payee only".
- **Copyright.** Writing is necessary for the transfer of copyright.
- **Existing equitable interests.** In order to transfer an existing equitable interest to another, the assignment must be in writing and signed by the assignor or his agent: s.53(1)(c) of the **Law of Property Act 1925**.

Failed Attempts

If the correct procedure is not followed, the transfer to the trustees will be ineffective. In *Richards v Delbridge* (1874), Mr Delbridge purported to transfer title to a lease. He wrote on the back of the lease "this deed and all thereto belonging I give to Edward Burnetto Richards from this time forth with all the stock in trade". The gift failed because there was no deed specifically created to effect the transfer. It could not be argued that Mr Delbridge had declared himself to be a trustee because he did not intend a trust to exist. He intended an outright gift. Similarly, in *Antrobus v Smith* (1806) an endorsement on the back of a share certificate was ineffective to pass title to the shares. Again, in

Re Fry (1946) a donor died after executing a share transfer, but (as he was resident abroad) he needed the consent of the Treasury to the transfer. He had not done this. Accordingly, the gift was ineffective.

WHEN WILL EQUITY ASSIST A VOLUNTEER?

A completely constituted trust is enforceable by all beneficiaries whether or not they have given consideration. An incompletely constituted trust can be enforced only by those beneficiaries who have given consideration. The imperfect transfer is then treated as a contract to transfer which may be specifically enforced. The principle that equity will not assist a volunteer may, however, be sidestepped in a number of ways. These are:

- the so-called every effort rule: *Re Rose* (1952);
- when it would be unconscionable for the donor to change his mind, as promoted by Arden L.J. in the *Pennington v Waine* (2002);
- donatio mortis causa, the rules which relate to deathbed gifts;
- in cases of fortuitous vesting (*Strong v Bird* (1874); *Re Ralli's Will Trust* (1964));
- proprietary estoppel.

The Every Effort Rule

DEFINITION CHECKPOINT

The "every effort doctrine" is an exception to the general rule that a transfer that fails at law will not take effect in equity. If the donor has done everything he can do to transfer the gift but its effectiveness depends on some act of a third party, the gift may not necessarily fail.

KEY CASES

RE ROSE (1952), MASCALL V MASCALL (1984) AND RE FRY (1946)

- In *Re Rose* (1952), the donor executed a share transfer form and handed it, together with the share certificate, to the donee. Although the transfer would not be complete until the shares had been registered by the company in the name of the donee, the gift was upheld. The donor had no more to do to perfect the gift.

- In *Mascall v Mascall* (1984) a father delivered an executed land transfer form and land certificate to his son. Following an argument, and before the transfer was registered, the father sought to withdraw from the transaction. It was held that the every effort rule applied and that it was too late to withdraw from the process.
- In *Re Fry* (1946) the problem was that the donor still had something to do himself and, therefore, had not made every effort. As was required in that case, he had not obtained Treasury consent to a transfer of shares.

Pennington v Waine

Some confusion has been caused by the Court of Appeal decision in *Pennington v Waine* (2002). There the donor signed the appropriate share transfer form in relation to 400 shares in a private company and gave it to her adviser to deal with. Prior to the donor's death, the adviser had written to the donee stating that he had been instructed to transfer the shares to the donee and inviting the donee to become a director of the company. The donee then signed a form agreeing to become a director and was assured that there was nothing else for him to do. No further action was taken by the adviser. On the donor's death, the issue arose as to whether the 400 shares formed part of the donor's residual estate or were, instead, held on trust for the donee, pending registration of the transaction. The latter argument prevailed. Arden L.J. took the view that the last step was taken by the donor when the court deems it to be unconscionable for the donor to renege on the gift. This is an unhelpful and questionable decision that flies in the face of well-established authority. The better view is that, unless some arrangement has been made for delivery of the transfer form, the donor truly cannot be said to have taken every step that he has to take. Ironically, on the facts of *Pennington* the court could simply have found that the adviser became an agent for the donor for the purpose of submitting the share transfer to the Company. Hence, arrangements for delivery had been made by the donor and there was no need to invoke the notion of unconscionability.

The Role of Unconscionability

In *Pennington v Waine* (2002), the Court of Appeal concluded that, on the facts, it would have been unconscionable for the donor to recall the gift once the donee had agreed to become a director. It followed, therefore, that it would be equally unconscionable for her personal representative to refuse to hand over the share transfer form to the donee. In those circumstances, delivery of the share transfer before the donor's death was unnecessary. Legal title was to remain vested in the donor's estate pending registration of the transaction.

During the intervening period, the donor's personal representative became the constructive trustee of the legal title to the shares for the donee.

Criticism

The prevailing view, however, is that the Court of Appeal adopted a very mistaken interpretation of previous authority. The key authority relied on (some might say hijacked) by the appellate court was the Privy Council decision in *T Choithram International v Pagarani* (2001). There, the settlor executed a deed of trust in which he nominated himself and nine others as trustees. He did not, however, transfer the title of the assets to the other trustees. Lord Browne-Wilkinson upheld the trust. The settlor had done enough to declare himself a trustee. It did not matter that he intended to be one of a number of trustees (and not a sole trustee). The Privy Council accepted that it would now be unconscionable for the settlor to renege on the declaration of trust. There was nothing to show that the settlor wanted the trust to come into effect only when all trustees had legal title. This is a very different scenario from that which faced the Court of Appeal in *Pennington v Waine* (2002) where there was neither a declaration of trust nor the making of a gift.

Donationes Mortis Causa (DMC)

> **DEFINITION CHECKPOINT**
>
> This exception refers to a lifetime gift made in contemplation of death. The central notion of a DMC is that a gift by reason of death may, in certain circumstances, be perfected even though the necessary formalities of transfer have not been followed. Since *Sen v Headley* (1991), any type of property can, seemingly, be the subject of DMC: cheques, chattels, shares (even if in a private company), bonds, insurance policies, land, etc. Not surprisingly, a number of conditions need to be satisfied before there can be a valid DMC.

The gift must have be made in contemplation of death

- Death must be thought by the donor to be imminent and more is required than a vague or general contemplation of death. In *Re Craven* (1937), it was said that the contemplation must be of "death within the near future".

- Death must also be contemplated from a source (e.g. illness, subsequent to an accident, suicide, fear of a crash). The gift will still be perfected if the deceased dies from a different cause than was anticipated. In *Wilkes v Arlington* (1931), the donor was dying of cancer and made a valid

DMC in contemplation of death, even though he eventually died of pneumonia.

- Contemplation can be expressed (i.e. the "if I die I want you to have this" style of case) or it can be inferred from the circumstances. In *Gardner v Parker* (1818), the connection between the gift and the contemplation of death was inferred from the fact that the donor was terminally ill when he made the gift and died shortly after the making of it.

The gift must be conditional on the death of the donor

- It was emphasised in *Cain v Moon* (1896), the gift must be made in circumstances that show that the property is to revert back to the donor if he recovers.
- The gift becomes absolute only on the donor's death and is revocable until that event occurs and ineffective if it does not: *Sen v Headley* (1991).
- There can be no DMC if the donor intends to make an immediate gift. In *Tate v Hilbert* (1793), the court held that the deceased had attempted to make an immediate and unconditional gift to his nieces and, hence, there could be no valid DMC.
- The condition can be express (e.g. "on my death this is yours") or readily inferred from the circumstances. *Gardner v Parker* (1818) suggests as a general rule that, if the gift is made in expectation of death, in the absence of contrary evidence it will be regarded as being conditional on the death of the donor.

Control and possession of the property must pass before death

- If delivery occurs after the donor's death, there will be no DMC: *Hardy v Baker* (1738).
- If the donee refuses to accept delivery there can be no DMC: *Cant v Gregory* (1894).
- Words alone do not suffice for these purposes. There must, therefore, either be actual and physical delivery of an item or symbolic delivery by the passing over of indicia of title to the item.
- The passing of keys to a locked safe can pass dominion over its contents. In *Woodward v Woodward* (1995), the passing over of keys to a car sufficed to pass dominion over the vehicle. In *Re Weston* (1902), the passing over of a savings book constituted passing dominion of the savings themselves. In *Sen v Headley* (1991), the handing over title deeds to house sufficed.

▌ DEFINITION CHECKPOINT

Simply put, the rule as to fortuitous vesting is that where there is a purported gift (including the forgiveness of a debt) to a donee, and the donee later happens to obtain legal title to the property in the capacity of executor under the donor's will, the gift will then be perfected: *Re Stewart* (1908). There is dubious authority to support that the rule applies equally where the donee is appointed an administrator on the intestacy of the donor: *Re James* (1935).

General observations

Although the rule has been explained in relation to gifts, it will apply equally to the transfer of property to trustees. Accordingly, if the trustee obtains legal title in the capacity of executor or administrator then the trust will be constituted and rendered effective. Equity is unconcerned with how the relevant title actually became vested in, say, the trustee. There are two types of fortuitous vesting, first under the rule in *Strong v Bird* (1874) and, secondly, under the contentious principle contained in *Re Ralli's Will Trusts* (1964).

Strong v Bird

Strong v Bird (1874) concerned a deceased creditor who had appointed her debtor as an executor under a will. The facts involved the release of a £1000 debt in favour of the debtor/executor and turned upon the presumed intention of the deceased. Even though there was no written release of the debt, the release was effective. Two conditions are present:

- the intention to forgive the debt/make the gift must continue until death: *Re Wale* (1956);
- there must be the intention to make an immediate release of the debt/ gift of the property. Accordingly, in *Re Freeland* (1952), the promise to give a car at a future date fell outside the rule.

Re Ralli's Will Trusts

In *Re Ralli's Will Trusts* (1964), a testator left his estate on trust for his wife for life and then for his daughter. Subsequently, the daughter entered into a covenant to transfer existing and after-acquired property to the trustees of her marriage settlement. The subsequent property referred to what was to come to her, following her mother's death, under her father's will. No transfer was ever made to her trustees. The daughter, however, predeceased the mother. On the mother's death, the trust property reverted back to the father's estate and title vested in the sole executor under the father's will. The executor was, by coincidence, also the remaining trustee under the daughter's marriage settlement. The fact that the trustee had title vested in him as executor perfected the otherwise imperfect trust.

Differences

This differs from *Strong v Bird* (1874) in that *Re Ralli's Will Trusts* (1964) is not limited to executors/administrators and, moreover, there is no need for continuing intention on the part of the donor. It is to be appreciated, however, that *Re Ralli's Will Trusts* has never been followed and real doubts are raised as to whether it is good law.

Proprietary Estoppel

> ### DEFINITION CHECKPOINT
>
> The doctrine of estoppel can be employed as a mechanism to perfect an otherwise imperfect gift or imperfectly constituted trust: *Thorner v Major* (2009). Estoppel operates to prevent the assertion of a party's strict legal rights in circumstances where it would be unconscionable for that party to rely on such rights. The key characteristics of proprietary estoppel are an express or implied **assurance** (which must be clear and certain: *Cobbe v Yeoman's Row* (2008)), **reliance** on that assurance and an associated **change of position/detriment**.

Satisfaction

Once an estoppel is invoked, it is for the court, in the exercise of a largely unfettered discretion, to decide how best it is to be satisfied. The claimant cannot, however, recover more than that which was assured. The court will examine matters in the round (i.e. assess the value of the representation, evaluate the extent of the detriment incurred, factor in any benefits already obtained and consider the conduct of the parties and the interests of others) and determine what remedy (if any) will be awarded: *Pascoe v Turner* (1979). In some cases, the court may order the donor to complete the gift or transfer (i.e. to perform the representation).

Illustrative cases

* In *Dillwyn v Llewelyn* (1862), a father assured his son that certain land now belonged to the son. The father did not, however, transfer the land to the son. The son then built a house on the land, but later the validity of the gift

was challenged. The son was able to invoke estoppel and compel the gift to be perfected.

- In *Jennings v Rice* (2002), the representation was that the claimant would be left a valuable property in the representor's will. Nevertheless, the court held that the extent of his detriment warranted instead a cash payment of £200,000.

Figure 4: Constitution of Trusts

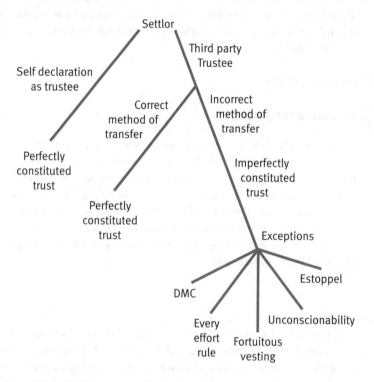

A Trust of the Benefit of a Covenant

DEFINITION CHECKPOINT

It is possible that a covenantor declares that the covenant to settle property (i.e. the promise itself) is the subject matter of the trust: *Fletcher v Fletcher* (1844). The trust would then be of the covenant and not, for example, the shares or the land which comprise the subject matter of the promise. In such cases, the beneficiaries will be able to enforce that trust because that trust will be perfectly constituted. They will have immediate equitable rights.

Limitations

Although it is perfectly permissible to create a trust of the benefit of a contract or a covenant, there are two potential limitations:

- The intention to make a trust of the promise (and not a trust of what is promised) must be clearly demonstrated: *Vandepitte v Preferred Accident Assurance Corp of New York* (1933). It is difficult to imagine a situation where the necessary intention could be inferred.
- It is debatable whether a trust of the covenant could cover after acquired property (e.g. shares acquired in the future). In *Re Cook's ST* (1965), the conclusion drawn was that it could not embrace such future property. Nevertheless, this runs contrary to traditional thinking and to the decision in *Davenport v Bishopp* (1843).

You should now know and understand:

- **what the constitution of a trust means;**
- **how trusts of different types of property may be constituted;**
- **the operation of the maxim "Equity will not assist a volunteer";**
- **the exceptional circumstances where Equity will assist a volunteer.**

QUESTION AND ANSWER

The Question

Chive told Garlic that he wanted her to hold some shares in a private company on trust for Marjoram and Thyme. He then telephoned the director of the company asking him to carry out the details of the transfer. The next day Chive was involved in an accident at his home. Marjoram and Thyme visited him. He told them of his conversation with Garlic and handed the share certificates to them. Unexpectedly, Chive died that night from his injuries. Garlic is the executor of Chive's will.

Advise Marjoram and Thyme.

In order to be enforceable a trust must be properly constituted either by the settlor making a declaration of trust or by transferring the trust property to trustees. A trust of shares can be declared orally, but an ineffective gift will not be construed as a declaration of a trust (*Jones v Lock*).

Chive has purported to transfer the shares to Garlic. There is no equity to perfect an imperfect gift. To transfer shares a share transfer form must be executed and the shares registered by the company in the name of the transferee. If, however, the transferor has done everything he needs to do, for example executing the transfer, but the effectiveness of the gift depends on a third party the gift will not fail (*Re Rose*). Where the transferor needs to take some further steps, like obtaining Treasury consent, the gift will not be effective (*Re Fry*). On the facts Chive has merely made a telephone call which is clearly insufficient.

Where a donor makes a gift in contemplation of imminent death (a donation mortis causa), equity may in some circumstances perfect what would otherwise be an imperfect gift. The gift must have been made in contemplation of imminent death. Here Chive died, but he did not make the gift because he expected to die. His immediate death was unanticipated. The handing over of the share certificates (even without a completed form of transfer) would, however, amount to sufficient delivery of the gift.

Marjoram and Thyme may be more successful under an extension of the rule in *Strong v Bird*. Where there is a continuing intention by the donor/settlor to make a gift and the property has been lawfully vested in the donee/trustee in another capacity (e.g. as the personal representative of the deceased) the gift/trust will then become effective. Accordingly, Garlic will be bound to hold the shares for Marjoram and Thyme.

The concept of unconscionability, as applied in *Pennington v Waine* would not operate here as it could not be said that it would be unconscionable for Chive to renege on the gift.

Formalities

5

INTRODUCTION

The general rule is that, once the three certainties are present, and legal title to the trust property is vested in the trustee, there is nothing more demanded of the settlor. By way of exception to this rule, however, Parliament has decreed that certain types of disposition require additional formalities before they can become effective. The most usual insistence is that the transaction either be in writing or, at the least, be evidenced (i.e. recorded) in writing and that such writing be signed. All testamentary dispositions (i.e. dispositions by will) are regulated by s.9 of the Wills Act 1837 whereas inter vivos trusts (i.e. lifetime trusts) are governed by s.53 of the **Law of Property Act 1925**.

WHY FORMALITIES?

Formalities are imposed primarily in order to protect the parties when property is held on trust. More specifically, the formality requirements are designed to:

- provide documentary evidence in order to minimise fraud;
- provide a provable record of transactions;
- instil certainty as to what the parties intended;
- establish the obligations of the trustee;
- deter secret transactions; and
- raise revenue for the Treasury by way of stamp duty.

TRUSTS CREATED BY WILL

DEFINITION CHECKPOINT

A will is a legal formal document which prescribes how a deceased's property is to be dealt with. A will has no legal significance until the death of the testator (will maker) and it can be revoked or revised at any stage prior to death. Provided that it is valid, a later version automatically replaces any earlier will. Marriage (but not divorce) also has an invalidating effect.

A testamentary disposition, whether by gift or by trust, must comply with s.9 of the **Wills Act 1837** (as amended). If it does not, the will fails and the gift or trust cannot take effect. Section 9 provides that a will shall not be valid unless:

- it is in writing;
- it is signed either by the testator or, alternatively, by some other person provided that it is made in the presence of and at the direction of the testator;
- the signature must be made or, alternatively, acknowledged by the testator in the presence of at least two witnesses present at the same time; and
- each witness must sign his name in the presence of the testator, but not necessarily in the presence of the other witness.

LIFETIME TRUST OF LAND

DEFINITION CHECKPOINT

Inter vivos trusts of land are subject to the additional formalities prescribed in s.53(1)(b) of the **Law of Property Act 1925**. This provides that, "a declaration of trust respecting any land or any interest therein must be manifested and proved by some writing signed by some person who is able to declare such a trust or by his will". These extra requirements are imposed because of both the value of land and the highly technical rules that attend its transfer.

Requirements

Section 53(1)(b) does not require that the trust be actually declared in writing, but does demand that a trust of land be evidenced in writing. The writing (which can be a will) can come into existence after the trust has been declared, but must contain all the terms of the trust: *Smith v Matthew* (1861). There is no prescribed form for this writing to take and it can span more than one document. The signature of the settlor is, however, required. There is no express mention made here of the ability of an agent to sign the document. The absence of writing does not make the trust void, but instead makes it unenforceable by a beneficiary: *Gardner v Rowe* (1828).

Exceptions

Section 53(1)(b) does not apply to resulting, implied or constructive trusts (s.53(2)). These types of implied trust are usually informal and exist to achieve fairness and to prevent unconscionable outcomes. Hence, to require formalities for the creation of such trusts would undermine the reason for their very existence.

Illustrative cases
- *Hodgson v Marks* (1971) where a widow was influenced by her lodger to transfer the title to her house into his name on the basis that this would prevent his eviction following her death. The lodger later sold the house to a third party. The Court of Appeal decided that the lodger had held the house on resulting trust for the widow and, as this implied trust fell outside s.53(1)(b), it was enforceable against the third party.
- *Bannister v Bannister* (1948) where two cottages were conveyed to the trustee on the basis that the beneficiary would be allowed to live in one of them for the rest of her life. The court would not allow the trustee to rely upon an absence of writing in these circumstances and invoked a constructive trust.
- *Rouchefoucald v Bousted* (1897) where there was a purely oral trust of land that was, at face value, unenforceable. As the claimant had acted to his detriment on the strength of this otherwise enforceable trust, the court felt that to fail to enforce the trust would amount to a fraud. The court, therefore, implied a constructive trust and sidestepped the need for formalities.

DEALING WITH AN EXISTING TRUST INTEREST

> **DEFINITION CHECKPOINT**
>
> Section 53(1)(c) of the **Law of Property Act 1925** provides that "a disposition of an equitable interest or trust subsisting at the time of the disposition, must be in writing signed by the person disposing of the same or by his agent thereunto lawfully authorised in writing or by will".

Initial Observations
- s.53(1)(c) applies only after a trust has been created. It has no relevance to the actual declaration of the trust under which the equitable interest arises. The formalities are designed to bite on the transfer of a subsisting equitable interest by a beneficiary to someone else or the direction of the beneficiary to the trustee to hold the trust property on behalf of another;
- the section applies to all property, that is, personal property as well as land;
- the formalities do not apply to resulting or constructive trusts: s.53(2);
- a failure to comply with s.53(1)(c) makes the transfer entirely void;

- the disposition (i.e. transfer) of the equitable interest itself has to be made in writing and not merely supported by documentary evidence. There is no scope here for any subsequent ratification in writing;
- for the purposes of writing, two interconnected documents can be read together in order to satisfy s.53(1)(c): *Re Danish Bacon Co Ltd Staff Pension Fund Trust* (1971); and
- the signature of an agent will suffice for the purposes of s.53(1)(c). This reflects the fact that such written assignments are unlikely to occur inadvertently.

Figure 5

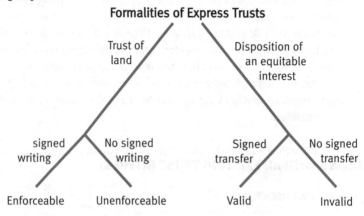

Formalities of Express Trusts

Section 53(1)(c): Key Cases

THE DIFFICULTY

Sometimes it is not clear whether a transaction amounts to a declaration of trust or is, instead, a disposition of an existing equitable interest. The cases appear inconsistent and illogical. This is because many of them are tax avoidance cases that involve the Inland Revenue. As dispositions have to be in writing, and writing attracts stamp duty, the Inland Revenue tends to argue for a disposition rather than a declaration. Stamp duty is charged on an instrument rather than on the transaction itself.

Grey v IRC (1960)

Facts: Mr Hunter transferred legal title in 18,000 shares to his trustees (one of whom was Mr Grey) to hold on an express, bare trust for himself. Shortly afterwards, Mr Hunter orally and irrevocably directed his trustees to hold those shares on trust for new beneficiaries (his grandchildren). The same trustees were the trustees of the grandchildren's pre-existing settlements. Mr Hunter attempted to do everything orally so as to escape liability for stamp duty. Subsequently, the trustees executed six documents confirming that they now held the shares on trust for the grandchildren. There was no doubt that the new trusts were valid. The issue was whether a direction by a settlor to his existing trustees to hold shares on trust for a third party fell within s.53(1)(c). In other words, did the equitable interest in the shares pass on the oral direction or subsequently on the trustees' written confirmation?

Outcome: The House of Lords had to consider what amounted to a disposition for the purposes of s.53(1)(c). It was held that a direction to trustees to hold on trust for another fell within s.53(1)(c) as it was a disposition of Mr Hunter's equitable interest. Put simply, Mr Hunter had held a subsisting equitable interest at the outset and now claimed to no longer hold such an interest. As the oral direction could not achieve this transfer, the documents executed by the trustees operated to effect the disposition. Stamp duty was, therefore, payable on those documents.

Oughtred v IRC (1960)

Facts: The trustees held shares for the benefit of Mrs Oughtred for life with remainder to her son, Peter. In return for some shares of his mother's, Peter made an oral contract to transfer his interest in remainder to her. Subsequently, formal transfers were executed transferring these shares to the mother. The Inland Revenue claimed stamp duty on the transfers as they were the documents that effectively transferred the interest. The House of Lords had to consider whether a formal transfer of shares following an oral agreement amounted to an assignment for the purposes of s.53(1)(c).

Outcome: It was contended that, by virtue of the doctrine of conversion that operates on a specifically enforceable contract, the equitable interest had already passed to the mother. Her case was, therefore, that the disposition of the equitable interest fell within the exception in s.53(2) because of the constructive sub-trust attendant to the contract. Hence, the writing transferred nothing. The majority of the House of Lords, however, rejected this argument. The contract did not pass the full equitable interest in the shares and, therefore, the document was subject to stamp duty. This appears to be a sensible conclusion as, if the contract was rescinded or specific performance ceased to be available, the entire equitable interest would have remained with the son.

Vandervell v IRC (1967)

Facts: A bank held shares on bare trust for Mr Vandervell. He directed the Bank to transfer the shares to the Royal College of Surgeons subject to an option to repurchase them for £5,000. The option was exercisable by the Vandervell trustees. The Inland Revenue mounted two alternative arguments. The first was that the transfer of the shares was caught by s.53(1)(c). This argument was destined to fail. Secondly, it was argued that the option to repurchase entailed that Mr Vandervell retained some equitable interest in the shares. This argument proved to be more fruitful for the Inland Revenue.

Outcomes:

(i) The House of Lords held that an oral direction by a beneficiary to trustees holding on a bare trust for him to transfer both the legal and the equitable interest to a third party will be effective. It was, however, important that here the legal and equitable ownership vested in one body (the Royal College of Surgeons). The outcome might have been much different if Mr Vandervell had attempted to move legal title one way and equitable title another.

(ii) The Inland Revenue, however, succeeded in establishing that Mr Vandervell had not divested himself of the equitable interest in the option to repurchase the shares. Although the legal title to the option was validly vested in the Vandervell trustees, no mention had been made of the equitable title. Accordingly, as the terms of the trusts had not been spelt out, there was a resulting trust to Mr Vandervell of the benefit of the option. Mr Vandervell was, therefore, liable to pay tax. As Lord Wilberforce pointed out, an equitable interest cannot exist in the abstract and must be vested somewhere.

Re Vandervell Trusts (No.2) (1974)

Facts: To continue the Vandervell saga, Mr Vandervell finally wanted to rid himself entirely of any interest that he had in the shares. In 1961, he instructed his trustees to exercise the option given to them and orally directed them to hold the shares so repurchased on trust for his children. The trustees used £5,000 from a trust fund already established to benefit Mr Vandervell's children. Subsequently, the dividends of those shares were transferred to the children's trust fund. In 1965, and to resolve any doubts, Mr Vandervell executed a deed of release by which he transferred to Vandervell Trustees Ltd his equitable interest in the shares, expressly declaring that the shares were to be held on trust for his children. Mr Vandervell died in 1967 and made no further provision for his children in the belief that they were well provided for under the trust. Later that year, the Inland Revenue claimed tax from his executors on the dividends that had been paid between 1962 and 1965 (£769,580 net).

Outcome: The dispute reached the Court of Appeal where it was held that there had been a valid declaration of trust by the trustees in 1961 when they exercised the option and this put the case outside s.53(1)(c). This declaration had the effect of terminating the resulting trust in favour of Mr Vandervell. Lord

Denning M.R. consolidated his decision by adding that, even if Mr Vandervell had retained a post-option equitable interest in the shares, he would have been estopped from asserting a claim against his children.

Grounds for criticism
- it is difficult to see how there could be a genuine declaration of trust by the company who already thought that it was a trustee;
- it is also difficult to understand why, as there was a resulting trust of the option, there was not also a resulting trust of the shares that resulted from the exercise of such option;
- the fact that the beneficial interest passed from Mr Vandervell to his children under their settlements looks more like a disposition than the declaration of a new trust; and
- the case for estoppel is a weak one. As regards the benefits afforded to the children, it is clearly disproportionate to the payment of £5,000 and well beyond the "minimum equity" normally afforded to successful claimants. It is also unclear what detriment (other than the payment of £5,000 which could easily be refunded) the children had suffered as a result of the representation that they were the beneficial owners of the shares.

SECTION 53(1)(C): FINAL THOUGHTS

The operation of s.53(1)(c) is complex and defies ready understanding. It is, therefore, helpful to list the key points concerning its application.
- It is the transfer/disposition of an existing equitable interest under a trust that has to be in signed writing.
- The transfer of the beneficial interest of one beneficiary to another requires writing (*Grey v IRC*). This is so whether the transfer takes the form of an assignment or a direction to trustees.
- Section 53(1)(c) does not apply when the entire legal and equitable interest in the property passes to a single entity (*Vandervell v IRC*). It is a dubious proposition to suggest that the section similarly does not apply where legal title moves one way and equitable title another in the same transaction.
- If a sub-trust is created under which the beneficiary retains some function and, thereby, does not dispose of the entire beneficial interest, the traditional understanding is that this sub-trust is beyond the reach of s.53(1)(c). If the sub-trust involves a complete disposal of the beneficial interest, however, it is thought that this requires a written transfer.

- It was recognised in *Re Vandervell (No.2)* that the interest under a resulting trust can be disposed of without the need for writing.
- It was also recognised in *Re Vandervell (No.2)* that, even though it is not specifically identified as an exception in s.53(2), an estoppel can circumvent the need for writing.
- As regards a contract to transfer both legal and equitable title in, say, land or shares in a private company, the constructive trust that arises does not pass the full beneficial interest to the purchaser (*Oughtred v IRC*).

Revision Checklist

You should now know and understand:

- **the reasons for additional formalities;**
- **the requirements for a valid will;**
- **the operation of s.53(1)(b) with reference to case law;**
- **the operation of s.53(1)(c) with reference to case law.**

QUESTION AND ANSWER

The Question

"Although the formalities imposed by s.53(1)(c) of the Law of Property Act 1925 are intended to promote certainty and to avoid fraud, as Mr Vandervell might testify the insistence upon writing may itself produce uncertainty and injustice".

Discuss this statement.

Advice and the answer

This is a standard style essay question which requires you to consider the operation of s.53(1)(c) with reference both to the quotation under discussion and the seminal cases which have tackled the meaning and application of this statutory provision. Although there is no set way of undertaking an essay, it is always useful to keep in mind that there should be a beginning, middle and end.

The beginning should make some reference to the quotation under discussion and set out the ingredients of s.53(1)(c). In particular, you should make clear that it only applies to a disposition of an existing trust interest and that it requires the disposition itself to be in signed writing. The writing then becomes a document of transfer and attracts what is commonly known as stamp duty. Indeed, the latter liability explains most attempts to transfer the trust interest orally.

The middle should look in detail at the key cases decided on s.53(1)(c). At the least, you should consider the decisions and arguments raised in *Grey*; *Vandervell (No.1)*; *Oughtred* and *Vandervell (No.2)*. You should emphasise the types of transaction to which the section applies and, importantly, those dispositions which fall outside its reach.

The end should apply the previously discussed decisions, arguments and distinctions with reference to the quotation under discussion. You should either agree or disagree with the quotation with reference to the option issue raised in *Vandervell (No.1)* and the controversial reasoning of Lord Denning in *Vandervell (No.2)*.

Secret Trusts

6

INTRODUCTION

Secret trusts are testamentary trusts that usually arise in circumstances where the settlor leaves a legacy in his will on the secret understanding that the legatee (a trusted person such as a solicitor) will hold that property on trust for a third party. The legacy may either appear to be absolute (as with a fully secret trust) or disclose the trust without revealing its object (as with a half secret trust).

THE PROBLEM?

The potential stumbling block is that, as shown in Chapter 5, testamentary dispositions (including trusts) must be executed and attested in compliance with the formalities prescribed in the **Wills Act 1837**. The key features of that prescription are, it is to be recalled, writing, signature and attestation. Although the general rule is that any purported legacy or testamentary trust which is not specified in a valid will be ineffective, the secret trust is an exception to this rule. The secret trustee cannot deny the trust on the ground of an absence of formality.

WHY SECRET TRUSTS?

The purpose of a secret trust is to keep the identity of the beneficiary undisclosed (e.g. the secret beneficiary is the testator's illegitimate child or mistress). This might be viewed as necessary because, once probate is granted, a will becomes a document of public record. It can be inspected by anyone who pays the appropriate fee. A further reason for using a secret trust is to allow any changes and future dispositions to be made without adherence to the Wills Act. A fully secret trust also affords flexibility for a testator who cannot quite make up his mind what to leave to whom. His instruction to his trustee might change several times before his death. As will become clear, the same flexibility does not apply to half secret trusts.

TWO TYPES OF SECRET TRUST

As mentioned, there are two types of secret trust: the fully secret trust and the half secret trust. It is crucial to understand this distinction because, in some situations, different rules apply to each. As to which category of secret trust has been created, it is necessary to look at the wording of the will.

A Fully Secret Trust

> **DEFINITION CHECKPOINT**
>
> A fully secret trust operates in circumstances where it appears from the face of the will that the legatee is entitled to take the legacy absolutely. No indication of a trust or its terms is, therefore, discernible from the will itself.

> **KEY CASE**
>
> **OTTAWAY V NORMAN (1972)**
> In *Ottaway v Norman* (1972), the testator agreed with his housekeeper that she could have his bungalow after his death provided that she, in turn, left it to the testator's son and daughter-in-law on her own death. She agreed to this and the testator left the bungalow to her absolutely. On her death, however, she left the property to another. The court held the son and daughter-in-law were entitled to the property.

Intestacy ·
It is also possible that a fully secret trust can arise on intestacy (where no will exists): *Sellack v Harris,* (1708). If an owner of property does not make a will because the person entitled on intestacy has agreed to hold it for a secret beneficiary then the trust should be enforceable: *Re Gardner* (1920).

A Half Secret Trust

> **DEFINITION CHECKPOINT**
>
> With a half secret trust, the existence of a trust is not secret (i.e. it is mentioned in the will), but it is the terms of the trust (particularly, the identity of the beneficiary) that will remain private and undisclosed. Take, for example, a provision that reads, "£500,000 for X to be held on trust for such purposes as I have communicated to him". The trust (but not its terms) is evident from the will itself.

Classification problems

There can sometimes be difficulty in classifying whether a trust is fully secret or half secret. For example, "£50,000 to X knowing that he will carry out my wishes as I have communicated to him". The problem is that the testator has used precatory words (see Chapter 3) that no longer import a trust. Accordingly, this should create a fully secret trust and not, as it may first appear, a half secret trust. In *Irvine v Sullivan* (1869), the wording of the will was "trusting that she will carry out my wishes with regard to the same, with which she is fully acquainted". This amounted to a fully secret trust.

JUSTIFICATION FOR SECRET TRUSTS

Although secret trusts form an exception to the formalities imposed by the Wills Act, little thought is given by the courts as to why secret trusts are treated differently. There has to be some justification for equity to override a statutory provision in this way. There are several schools of thought as to what is the underlying rationale for the law relating to secret trusts. Unfortunately, none of them is entirely satisfactory.

FRAUD

The traditional explanation for the enforcement of secret trusts is that they exist in order to prevent fraud. As to fully secret trusts, if the legatee/trustee attempts to keep the property for himself this will be a clear fraud. In such a scenario, unless evidence is admitted contrary to the provisions of the **Wills Act**, the intended trustee will profit from his misconduct. As such, the justification for recognising the fully secret trust is easily made out.

And half secret trusts?

In relation to half secret trusts, however, this reasoning is inapplicable. If the court refused to admit evidence of the terms of the trust, the trustee could not take the property himself, but would instead hold it on resulting trust for the testator's estate. As the trustee will not profit from the failure of the trust, it is more difficult to speak in terms of there being a fraud. It might be argued that the fraud is committed on both the testator and the beneficiary if the trust is not upheld. There is, however, no real fraud on the beneficiary who loses out simply because the settlor did not adhere to the prescribed formalities for creating a testamentary trust. As shown in Chapter 5, equity is not prepared to act in this tolerant fashion in relation to a non-compliance with s.53(1)(b) and (c) of the **Law of Property Act 1925**.

Dehors the Will

A more modern view canvassed is that a secret trust (whether fully secret or half secret) operates "dehors" (i.e. outside) the will: *Blackwell v Blackwell* (1929). In other words, the trust arises not from the will, but from its lifetime communication to, and acceptance by, the trustee. Communication and acceptance operate to impose personal obligations on the trustee. The trust, however, only becomes constituted on the testator's death (i.e. the property vests in the trustee by virtue of the settlor's will). Accordingly, the claim that the trust operates entirely outside the will is a fictitious one.

KEY CASE

RE YOUNG (1951)

In *Re Young* (1951) the testator made a bequest to his wife with a direction that on her death she should leave £2,000 for their chauffeur. Although the chauffeur had witnessed the will, he was still entitled to the money. The legacy was not void under s.15 of the **Wills Act** which is designed to prevent a witness to a will being a beneficiary under it. Danckwerts J. promoted the dehors theory, "The whole theory of the formation of a secret trust is that the **Wills Act 1837** has nothing to do with the matter".

Incorporation by Reference

The least attractive theory is that the doctrine of incorporation by reference offers the true justification underlying the recognition of half secret trusts. Fully secret trusts are justified on the fraud theory discussed above. The doctrine of incorporation is one of probate law and allows incorporation of a written document into a will when the will specifically refers to it. For example, the will might state "I leave Blackacre to X on the trusts which I have communicated to him by a letter dated May 2, 2009". This letter may then be admitted to probate together with the will. As the will must refer to the document to be incorporated, the document must be in existence prior to the will: *Johnson v Ball* (1851). If not, there can be no incorporation.

A flawed theory?

Incorporation by reference is largely discredited as offering the basis of the half secret trust. The difficulties with it are that secret trusts need not be declared in a document (they can be oral), that the trust entirely loses its secrecy (i.e. the document is admitted into probate with the will and is open for public inspection) and that it would need to be communicated to the trustee before the will is executed. The incorporation theory stands in contradiction to key authorities (whether they point in favour of the fraud or the dehors theories).

THE CREATION OF A SECRET TRUST

Ingredients

In *Ottaway v Norman* (1972), Brightman J. outlined the three vital ingredients of a secret trust:

- the intention of the testator to subject the primary donee to an obligation in favour of the secondary donee;
- the communication of that intention to the primary donee; and
- the acceptance of that obligation by the primary donee either expressly or by acquiescence.

Intention

The Court of Appeal in *Kasperbauer v Griffith* (2000) demonstrated that a secret trust (of whatever category) requires certainty of intention that it is a trust that is to be created. There a statement that his wife "knew what she had to do" was equivocal and sufficient only to impose a moral (i.e. not legal) obligation on the wife. Similarly, in *McCormick v Grogan* (1869) the testator wrote a letter which read, "I do not wish you to act strictly to the foregoing instructions, but leave it entirely to your own good judgment to do as you think I would if living, and as the parties are deserving". This again did not reveal the intention to create a secret trust and, therefore, the legatee could keep the money absolutely.

Communication

As regards both a fully secret trust and a half secret trust, it is crucial that the obligation to hold the property on trust and the terms of the trust (including the subject matter and its beneficiaries) be communicated to the trustee. For example, when there is more than one beneficiary, the identity of all the beneficiaries and their entitlements under the secret trust will need to be divulged to the trustee. If, as in *Ottaway v Norman* (1972), the trustee is to be given a life interest in the property then this must be communicated to the secret trustee.

Forms of communication

Communication can be oral or take the form of a letter, fax, text message, sign language or email. Communication can also occur via the testator's agent. It is, moreover, possible that communication of the terms of the trust can be constructive. The classic example is *Re Keen* (1937) where the testator made his will and this disclosed the existence of a secret trust relating to the sum of £10,000. The trustee was handed a sealed envelope that contained the name of the secret beneficiary. The letter was not to be opened until after the death of the testator. The Court of Appeal drew the parallel with a ship sailing under sealed orders where the exact terms are not ascertained until later. The trustee

Figure 6: Secret Trusts

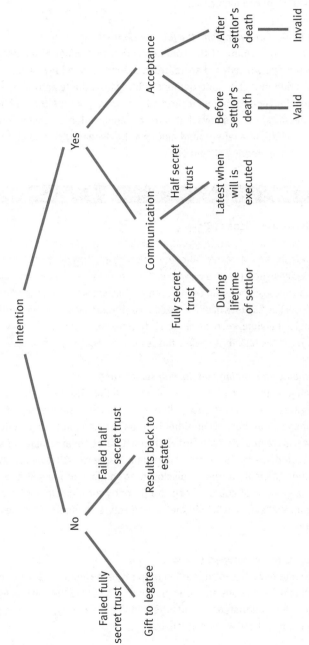

has the means of ascertaining the identity of the beneficiary and this amounts to a sufficient communication.

Communication timing and the fully secret trust

It is as to the timing of the communication that major differences emerge between the two styles of secret trust. In relation to a fully secret trust, communication must be made during the lifetime of the testator (i.e. it must be made inter vivos). Communication may, however, occur either before or after the will is drafted. It follows that, if the communication is subsequent to death (e.g. by virtue of a letter found amongst the deceased's papers), the legatee can take the property absolutely.

KEY CASE

WALLGRAVE V TEBBS (1855)

In *Wallgrave v Tebbs* (1855), the testator left £12,000 in his will jointly to Mr Tebbs and Mr Martin. After the testator's death, a draft letter was found specifying how the testator wanted them to hold the money. The court held that, because there had been no communication of this to Tebbs and Martin before the testator's death, there could be no binding trust. Tebbs and Martin could, therefore, keep the money. If, however, the trust had been communicated in the testator's lifetime the secret trust would have been effective.

Communication timing and the half secret trust

Although communication must still occur before the death of the testator, as regards a half secret trust a different dimension is added and this is that communication must occur either before the will or, at the very latest, when the will is created: *Re Keen* (1937). If communication takes place after the will is executed, the half secret trust must fail: *Blackwell v Blackwell* (1929). As the intention to create a trust is disclosed on the face of the will, the intended trustee cannot, of course, keep the property for himself: *Re Boyes* (1884). Instead, the legatee will hold the property on resulting trust for the testator's estate.

Increases to trust property

If the testator wishes to add further property to the intended secret trust, these additional instructions must also be communicated to the trustee. A failure to do so will entail that, as regards the additional property, the secret trust will fail with the following consequences:

*   if it is a fully secret trust, the legatee will be able to keep the excess amount;

- if it is a half secret trust, the additional property will be held on resulting trust for the deceased's estate. In *Re Colin Cooper* (1939), the testator left £5,000 to trustees on terms that he had already communicated to them. Without the knowledge of the trustees, however, he increased the sum to £10,000 by codicil (i.e. a formal and attested variation of the will). It was held that the trustees held the initial £5,000 on the terms of the trust, but that the remaining £5,000 resulted back to the deceased's estate. As regards the latter sum, there had simply been no communication and acceptance of the revised terms of the trust.

Acceptance

The rules concerning the acceptance by the legatee of the obligations of trusteeship are the same whether it is a fully secret trust or half secret trust. Acceptance can be made at any time before the testator's death. The acceptance of trusteeship can arise in one of two ways, i.e. by express agreement or by implication from silence. Silence, in this context, amounts to tacit acceptance: *Paine v Hall* (1812). The key is whether the trustee's conduct induced the testator to make the legacy and pursue the arrangement of a secret trust. This is because equity will not allow a man to profit by his fraud. It is open for a person to refuse to act or, indeed, to continue to act as a secret trustee.

More than one secret trustee?

There are potential difficulties if the gift is to two legatees and only one has accepted the trust. The outcome may differ according to whether it is a fully secret trust or a half secret trust.

With a fully secret trust, much turns upon whether the legatees are joint tenants or tenants in common. If the former, both will hold on trust whereas, if the latter, the trust would bind only the party that undertook the obligation: *Re Stead* (1901). The other will be able to keep his legacy.

With a half secret trust, the trustees always hold as joint tenants and so both legatees should be bound.

PREDECEASING THE TESTATOR

If the Trustee Dies First?

In circumstances where a fully secret trust is intended, but the sole secret trustee dies before the testator, the legacy lapses and the property will remain in the testator's estate: *Re Maddock* (1902). If, however, other trustees survive the testator, the trust should remain valid in relation to the entire property. As regards half secret trusts, however, it is thought that the death of the sole trustee will not prevent the trust from taking effect because of the rule that equity will not allow a trust to fail for want of a trustee: *Re Armitage* (1972).

If the Beneficiary Dies First?

In the situation where the secret beneficiary predeceases the testator, the secret trust must fail. It comes into effect via the will, which in turn comes into effect on the death of the testator. If at that time, the beneficiary is no longer living, there can be no trust. The testamentary trust will, therefore, be frustrated in the same way as would occur with an inter vivos trust: *Re Corbishley's Trusts* (1880).

Revision Checklist

You should now know and understand:

- **what is a secret trust and why is it problematic?**
- **the distinction between half secret and fully secret trusts;**
- **the conditions necessary for the existence of a valid secret trust;**
- **the theories underpinning the existence of secret trusts.**

QUESTION AND ANSWER

The Question

On November 29, Malcolm told Jane that if she agreed, he wanted her to act as his trustee, holding on behalf of Nathan. On December 1, Malcolm made his will leaving his home, Dunborin, and £100,000 to Jane "on such trusts as I have indicated to her" and the residue of his estate to Hollis. On December 2 Malcolm handed Jane a sealed envelope saying that the contents confirmed their conversation of November 29, but that it was only to be opened upon his death. The letter, when opened, stated that Dunborin and the £100,000 were to be held on trust for Nathan.

    Advise Jane.

Advice and the answer

Malcolm's will leaves his home Dunborin and £100,000 to Jane as trustee. This may create a half secret trust. It is not a fully secret trust as the trust (but not its terms) is evident from Malcolm's will. There is no possibility of Jane taking the property beneficially. Jane will either hold the property on trust for Nathan if a half-secret trust can be established or, if not, for Hollis (who is entitled to Malcolm's residuary estate).

Before a half secret trust will be valid the following must be established:

- there must be sufficient communication of the terms of the trust before or at the same time as the will. The rule is based on *Blackwell v Blackwell*, but has been severely criticised. cf. fully secret trusts where the trustee appears to take beneficially on the face of the will, communication can take place at any time before the testator's death;
- there must be acceptance of the terms by the trustee;
- there must be no conflict between the terms of the will and the secret trust.

It is impossible to tell from the facts whether there was a sufficient communication on November 29. To be effective, Jane must have been told of the property to be comprised in the trust (*Re Colin Cooper*). If not, the subsequent letter will not be a sufficient communication. Although communication can take place in a sealed envelope, provided the trustee knows it contains the terms of the trust (*Re Keen*), in this case it will be ineffective as the letter is given a day after the will.

Jane can accept the trust by implication (e.g. by silence: *Paine v Hall*). It appears that there is no conflict between the will and the terms of the trust that are alleged to have been communicated on November 29. If, however, communication is by the letter of December 2 (after the will) then it is not only too late, but there is also a conflict with the will because at that stage nothing had been communicated.

The Statutory Avoidance of Trusts

7

INTRODUCTION

Unless there is a power of revocation in the trust instrument, the general rule is that, once a trust has been completely constituted, it cannot be revoked by the settlor or, indeed, by anyone else. Unless the settlor is also a trustee, the trust property moves outside his legal control. Real ownership has become vested in the beneficiaries. This general rule is, subject to a number of statutory exceptions under which the court can set aside a gift or transfer to a trustee. Put broadly, these powers arise in the context of transactions to put property unfairly beyond the reach of creditors, spouses and family. It is with these statutory exceptions that this Chapter is concerned.

TRANSACTIONS DEFRAUDING CREDITORS

Context

Settlors may attempt to employ the trust as a means of putting property beyond the grasp of potential creditors. The transfer of property to trustees on trust for named family members generally has the effect of negating the settlor's interest in those assets and putting them potentially beyond the reach of his creditors. The settlor's attitude is described by Jessell M.R. in *Re Butterworth* (1882), "If I succeed in business, I make a fortune for myself. If I fail, I leave my creditors unpaid. They will bear the loss". Although the law strives to let a person do what he wants with his own property, Parliament has taken steps to protect creditors from the consequences of this type of debt evasion. Outside such legislative restrictions, however, a trust can be employed effectively to sidestep a creditor's claims. Indeed, the use of offshore trusts (often situated in the Channel Isles) is usually to achieve the protection of assets against adverse claims, whether by a private creditor or HM Revenue & Customs.

General Protection for Creditors

The present law is to be found within the Insolvency Act 1986. This gives to the court a jurisdiction to set aside transactions that are at an undervalue and which operate unfairly to disadvantage creditors. As will become clear, albeit with some modifications, the jurisdiction applies whether or not the settlor has been adjudged bankrupt.

Other than on the bankruptcy of the debtor, a transaction at an undervalue may only be set aside under the auspices of ss.423–425 of the **1986 Act**. Under these provisions there is no need that the transferor be insolvent. There is, moreover, no requirement that a debt exists at the time of the transaction. As in *Re Butterworth* (1882), a businessman might make a settlement in favour of his wife prior to embarking upon a risky business venture, with a view to putting the property beyond the claims of future creditors. The transaction is clearly vulnerable to being set aside. In addition, there is no time limit beyond which the transaction is immune for these purposes.

Conditions

There are three conditions underlying the s.423 jurisdiction:

- the transaction has to involve an undervalue;
- the purpose of the transaction must be either to place assets beyond the reach of a person who is making, or may in future make, a claim against the settlor or to prejudice in some other way the interests of such a person in relation to any present or future claim made against the settlor;
- the claimant must demonstrate that he is a victim of the transaction and this is adjudged as at the time of the application and not the transfer. While the victim will usually be a creditor of the transferor, it could be a non-creditor who is in litigation with the transferor or who has a cause of action against the transferor.

What is an undervalue?

By virtue of s.423(1), an undervalue is the making of a gift, entering into a transaction in consideration of marriage or entering into a transaction for consideration which, in terms of money or money's worth, is "significantly less than" the equivalent value of the property transferred. In *Agricultural Mortgage Corp v Woodward* (1995), a farmer's land was mortgaged to the AMC. He granted a tenancy to his wife so that the mortgagee would not be able to sell the land with vacant possession. Although the wife paid a full market rent, this was treated as a transaction at an undervalue and was set aside. The real benefit acquired by the wife was much greater than the rent she paid because she was in a position to demand a ransom for surrendering her tenancy so as to make the farm available to the creditor.

Purpose

There is no requirement that the settlor must act dishonestly. A transaction can be impugned even if the settlor was acting on legal advice. It is not even necessary that a s.423 purpose be the predominant motive underlying the transaction. For example, in *IRC v Hashmi* (2002) the fact that it was also the intention of the settlor to benefit a family member did not prevent the operation of s.423. In *Moon v Franklin* (1990), the necessary intention was shown where a husband, threatened with legal proceedings, made substantial gifts to his wife from the proceeds of the sale of his business. It suffices that the ambition of the transferor is to deprive creditors of speedy access to property that would otherwise be applicable for their benefit.

Inferred intention

In certain circumstances, the intention to put assets beyond the creditor's reach will readily be inferred by the court. As Schiemann L.J. put it in *Barclays Bank Plc v Eustice* (1995),

> "when action by the creditor was clearly anticipated by the debtor and that these transfers were at an undervalue and that what remains in the hands of the debtor barely if at all covers the debt, there is in my judgment a strong prima facie case that the purpose of the transactions was to prejudice the interests of the creditor".

Figure 7

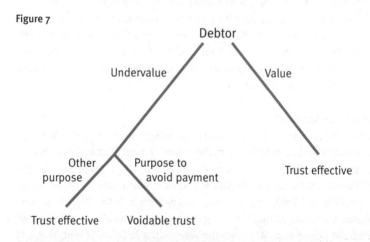

AND THIRD PARTIES?

To be effective, it is necessary that the powers of the court can be exercised against third parties. This is acknowledged in s.425(2) which states that an order made may affect the property of, or impose an obligation on, a third party whether or not that person was a party to the impugned transaction. Obviously, the immediate transferee is most at risk from the transaction being overturned. As regards subsequent transferees, however, they are protected provided that the transaction was entered in good faith, for value and without notice of the circumstances which made s.423 applicable in the first place. The same defence is available to a person who has acquired a benefit under the impugned transaction.

SPECIAL BANKRUPTCY PROVISIONS

The **Insolvency Act 1986** contains a number of further provisions that operate on the bankruptcy of a debtor and which enable the court to set aside transactions made at an undervalue (s.339) or by way of preference (s.340). The basic aim is to facilitate the trustee in bankruptcy in recovering the bankrupt's property for the benefit of creditors. These provisions apply only to transactions within a limited period before insolvency and the intention of the insolvent is irrelevant. They coexist with those dealing with undervalue transactions independently of bankruptcy. As will become clear, the two sets of provisions are similar, but are not identical.

Undervalue

Undervalue is given the same definition as considered above. As in *Re Densham* (1975), a trustee in bankruptcy of a husband may claim a wife's share in the matrimonial home to the extent that she did not contribute towards its purchase. The **Insolvency Act** also caters for a property adjustment order made in divorce proceedings to be overturned by one party's trustee in bankruptcy. There is a rebuttable presumption of undervalue where the transaction was entered into with an associate. An associate includes a spouse, relative, partner and employer.

Time limits

Certain time limits are imposed in relation to undervalue transactions by a bankrupt:

- two years. If a bankruptcy petition is presented within two years of any such transaction, then an order can be made in respect of it notwithstanding that the individual was solvent at the time;
- five years. If a bankruptcy petition is presented within five years of any such transaction, then an order can be made in respect of it unless the individual can prove that he was solvent at the time without the property included in the transaction.

Preference

A preference arises where the debtor places one of his creditors or a guarantor in a more favourable position, should the debtor's bankruptcy ensue, than would otherwise have been the case. It strikes at a transaction that improves the position of one creditor above those of others. The intention especially to benefit one creditor is a rebuttable presumption when the preference is given to an associate (see above).

Time limits

Certain time limits operate in relation to a preference:

- six months. The court can make an order concerning a preference given in the six months preceding the bankruptcy petition unless the individual was solvent at the time without the property included in the preference;
- two years. Where the preference is given to an associate, the court can make an order relating to a preference given in the two years preceding the bankruptcy petition unless the individual was (discounting the property included in the preference) solvent at the time.

Figure 8

FAMILY CLAIMS

It is possible that a transaction is designed to place property outside the grasp of a spouse, registered same sex partner or other dependant. Statutory restrictions have been imposed on the ability of a transferor to avoid maintenance and to avoid claims for financial provision. Two incursions upon the freedom of a property owner to deal with property are to be found in the Matrimonial

Causes Act 1973 and the Inheritance (Provision for Family and Dependants) Act 1975. The former applies to claims made in the course of matrimonial proceedings whereas the latter concerns the rights of dependants upon the death of the person who provided for them.

Marital Breakdown

Section 37 of the Matrimonial Causes Act 1973 allows transactions (including the declaration of a trust) to be set aside on the breakdown of a marriage. This can occur where the court is satisfied that one spouse has made a disposition with the intention of depriving the other of financial relief under the Act. The requisite intention will be presumed when the transaction occurs within three years preceding the other spouse's application for financial relief. The court can set aside a disposition unless it was made in favour of a bona fide purchaser for value without notice of any intention to defeat the applicant's claim: *Green v Green* (1981). By virtue of the Civil Partnership Act 2004, the same power operates on the dissolution of a same sex registered partnership.

Inheritance Provisions

In order to ensure that a surviving spouse (or same sex registered partner) and/or surviving dependants are provided for, the Inheritance (Provision for Family and Dependants) Act 1975 gives the court a broad, discretionary jurisdiction to make an award to a claimant. Section 2 empowers the court to allocate part of the deceased's estate to make reasonable financial provision for a surviving spouse registered, former spouse registered partner who has not remarried entered new partnership, cohabitant, child or other person who was, at the time of the death, maintained wholly or partly by the deceased. The order overrides the provisions a will or the operation of the intestacy rules.

Factors

The court is directed by s.3 to a number of factors which it must take into account. These include:

- the present and future financial resources and needs of the applicant;
- any obligations and responsibilities which the deceased owed to the applicant;
- the size and nature of the estate;
- the conduct of the parties; and
- any physical and mental disability of the applicant.

And third parties?

Sections 10 and 11 of the 1975 Act cater for the possibility that the deceased may have given away property prior to death with the intention of not providing for his spouse and dependants. The court is given the power to require the donee to make available a sum of money up to, but not in excess of, the value of the gift received. This power, however, arises only when the gift was made within six years before the donor's death and was made with the intention of defeating an application for financial provision under the 1975 Act. In Re Dawkins (1986), a husband left his entire estate to his daughter. He had also made a lifetime transfer of the matrimonial home to her for £100. His widow made a successful claim under the 1975 Act.

Revision Checklist

You should now know and understand:

- **the relevant provisions of the Insolvency Act 1986;**
- **the differences between a transaction at an undervalue and a preference;**
- **the special bankruptcy provisions;**
- **the family provisions.**

QUESTION AND ANSWER

The Question

To what extent has Parliament intervened to protect a creditor against a debtor utilising a trust in order to put assets beyond that creditor's reach?

Advice and the answer

This straightforward essay question requires a consideration of how a trust might be deployed to sidestep the legitimate claims of a creditor. It also requires the examination of the provisions of the Insolvency Act 1986 that apply (i) other than on bankruptcy and (ii) on bankruptcy.

As regards (i) it is necessary to explain the operation of s.423 in relation to undervalue transactions. The conditions underpinning this provision must be recited and, with illustrations from decided cases, the meaning of undervalue discussed. The essay should also refer to the courts' powers exercisable against third party.

In relation to (ii), the bankruptcy provisions contained in s.339 and s.340 need to be examined. Again there is required a brief explanation of undervalue and a discussion of what amounts to a preference. The different timing elements associated with both should also feature in the answer.

Resulting Trusts

8

The resulting trust is a type of implied trust that arises by operation of law. Accordingly, it is not expressly created by a settlor and there are no formal requirements for its creation. Following the speech of Lord Browne-Wilkinson in *Westdeutsche Landesbank v Islington LBC* (1996), the modern view is that the resulting trust arises in two principal contexts:

- failed trusts, where has been an attempt to create a trust and some part of the beneficial interest has not been entirely dealt with. Traditionally these are styled automatic resulting trusts;
- apparent gifts, where there is a voluntary transfer of property or a contribution to the purchase price of property without an express indication as to how equitable title is to be held. These are traditionally described as presumed intention resulting trusts.

Figure 9

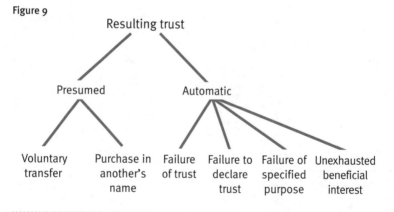

FAILED TRUSTS

> **DEFINITION CHECKPOINT**
>
> Where an express trust fails to dispose of the entirety of the beneficial interest, the remainder is held by implication on resulting trust for the settlor. The purpose of the resulting trust in this context is to restore

person continues to hold an equitable interest in the property. This may arise where there is:

- a failure to declare a trust;
- a failure of a trust;
- a failure of a specific purpose; and
- an unexhausted beneficial interest.

Failure to Declare a Trust

Where property is conveyed to persons with the intention that they act as trustees, the failure to declare the manner in which all of the beneficial interest is to be held on trust will entail that any property unaccounted for is held on resulting trust for the settlor. In *Vandervell v IRC* (1967), the beneficial interest in an option to repurchase shares was not dealt with. It was held that a resulting trust of the benefit of the option arose in favour of the settlor. The beneficial interest had to rest in someone and was not deemed to have been abandoned.

Failure of a Trust

This can occur for a variety of reasons.

- If the settlor has conveyed property on trust for A for life, and made no other provision, on A's death the property would result back to the settlor or the settlor's estate.
- Where a settlor conveys property on trust for A for life and then to A's children absolutely, but A never has children, the remainder will result back to the settlor. As there was the intention to create a trust, in both cases A or his estate cannot take the property as a gift.
- Where the trust turns out to be void because it is against public policy, advances an illegal purpose or offends the perpetuity rule.
- Consequent to the failure of a condition precedent (e.g. that X must marry, but X fails to marry) or condition subsequent (e.g. where the beneficiaries must remain married but they fail to do so). Accordingly, when a transfer of property is made subject to a condition which is not achieved the resulting trust effects a return of the property to the transferor.

KEY CASES

RE DIPLOCK (1951) AND RE ATKINSON'S WILL TRUSTS (1978)

In *Re Diplock* (1951), there was a gift of residue in a will "for purposes which the trustees consider to be charitable". This was not exclusively charitable and was, therefore, a private purpose trust that failed. The property resulted back to the settlor's estate and could be claimed by the grasping relatives.

In *Re Atkinson's Will Trusts* (1978), the uncertainty was found in a residuary gift which was to be divided between "such worthy causes as have been communicated by me to my trustees in my lifetime". As no such causes had been communicated, a resulting trust arose.

Failure of a Specific Purpose

This refers to cases where the transferor intends that the property revert back to him unless it is used for the particular purpose specified. In *Barclays Bank v Quistclose Investments Ltd* (1970), Quistclose paid money to Rolls Razor on the basis that the money would be used solely for a specified purpose (i.e. paying a dividend to shareholders) and that it would be deposited in a separate account. Rolls Razor became insolvent before any dividends were paid. The House of Lords held unanimously that the money advanced was held on resulting trust for Quistclose on the basis that the purpose for which it had been advanced had not been carried into effect.

Unexhausted Beneficial Interests

Different outcomes occur in different contexts. It is important to consider whether a trust is private or charitable in nature and whether a surplus arises from a desire to maintain individuals, carry out public appeals or in the event of the dissolution of unincorporated associations or the winding up of a pension fund.

KEY CASE

RE COCHRANE (1955)

In Re Cochrane (1955), a post-nuptial settlement was created into which both husband and wife brought property. In essence, the income generated was to be paid to the wife on the condition that she continued to reside with her husband. Should either die, the other would be entitled to the entirety beneficially. A problem arose when the wife left her husband and he died shortly thereafter. It was held that a resulting trust of the income arose in favour of the settlors in proportion to their contributions. Harman J. described the resulting trust as, "the last resort to which the law has recourse when the draftsman has made a blunder or failed to dispose of that which he has set out to dispose of".

Maintenance cases

The general rule is that a resulting trust will arise in respect of any surplus remaining once the purposes of the trust have been carried out. No resulting trust will arise where the trust instrument explicitly excludes this possibility or where an inference can be drawn that some other person was intended to take the property beneficially: *Westdeutsche Landesbank Girozentrale v Islington LBC* (1996)

KEY CASES

RE TRUSTS OF THE ABBOTT FUND (1900), RE ANDREWS TRUST (1905) AND RE OSOBA (1979)

- In *Re Trusts of the Abbott Fund* (1900), Dr Fawcett collected a sum of money, raising subscriptions from the public, to assist two women who were deaf and dumb. No provision was made as to the disposal of any surplus. Following the death of the two women, Stirling J. held that the subscriptions were never intended to be an absolute gift to them and that a resulting trust arose in favour of those who donated the money.
- In *Re Andrews Trust* (1905), money was subscribed "for or towards" the education of the infant children of a deceased clergyman. On the completion of their education, the children were entitled to all the money in equal shares. The court ascribed the broadest possible meaning to "education" and held that the overriding goal of benefiting the children could still be reached.
- In *Re Osoba* (1979) where a gift was made to the testator's widow "for the training of my daughter Abiola up to university grade". The daughter completed her education and a surplus remained. It was held that daughter was entitled to the entire fund. The reference to "education" was merely an explanation of the motive for the gift. Megarry J. felt that where the beneficiary is alive the courts should be reluctant to generate any other outcome.

Disaster funds

In *Re Gillingham Bus Disaster Fund* (1958), a fund was set up following a disaster arising from a bus accident. The collection was for the injured survivors who were all naval cadets. The government later declared that it would take over responsibility for the welfare of the cadets so that the purpose of the trust failed. It was held that the surplus money must result back to the subscribers. If the donors could not be found, the money was to be paid bona vacantia to the crown.

KEY CASE

RE WEST SUSSEX CONSTABULARY'S TRUST (1971)

In *Re West Sussex Constabulary's Trust* (1971), money was received from donations, collecting boxes and proceeds from entertainment events and was to be used to benefit the widows and dependants of deceased members of the West Sussex Constabulary. The money was held by an unincorporated association which was eventually wound up, leaving surplus funds. It was held that:

- money from identifiable donations should go back on a resulting trust;
- money from collecting boxes was an outright gift by the donors and, as there could be no resulting trust, inevitably must go to the Crown as bona vacantia;
- the proceeds of the entertainment events should also go bona vacantia. Those who had purchased tickets had received what they had paid for and there was no question of them claiming the money back.

Unincorporated associations

Unlike companies, unincorporated associations lack legal personality and cannot hold property in their own name. Consequently, difficulties arise as to how such societies hold their property and what happens to it on dissolution of the association. Three differing approaches have enjoyed prominence.

Resulting trust approach

A resulting trust was thought to arise in *Re Printers and Transferrers Amalgamated Trades Protection Society* (1899), where the unexpended funds of a society were redistributed on resulting trust principles. Division was in accordance with the amounts contributed by the existing members. This principle was followed in *Re Hobourn Aero Components Limited's Air Raid Disaster Fund* (1946), where it was held that any contributor to the disaster fund was entitled to an interest in the surplus under a resulting trust in proportion to the amount contributed, but subject to any adjustment made on the basis of a benefit derived from the fund. This approach is no longer in favour.

Bona vacantia

The surplus may go to the Crown bona vacantia. In *Cunnack v Edwards* (1895), financial contributions to a society, made in order to provide annuities for the widows of its deceased members, were viewed as an out-and-out transfer (i.e. a gift). On the dissolution of the society, there was no one to whom the surplus could go to by way of resulting trust. The members had received everything to which they were entitled and the surplus went to the Crown as bona vacantia. Bona vacantia is the option pursued in the case of a moribund society (where all, or all but one of the members have died).

Contract holding theory

The funds may be distributed between the members in accordance with the contract holding theory. The prime example of this is *Re Bucks Constabulary Fund (No.2)* (1979) where Walton J. held that the distribution of property on dissolution was to be governed by the contract between the members. Walton J. saw no residuary role for the resulting trust. Where the rules of the association are silent as to what should happen on dissolution, there is a presumption of equal division amongst the existing members. The modern tendency is to treat the rights of the members as being of a contractual nature without imposing a resulting trust: *Re Recher* (1972).

Over funded pensions

In *Davis v Richards and Wallington Industries Ltd* (1990), Scott J. considered the winding up of a pension fund that contained contributions from three specific sources: those of employers, those of employees and money transferred from other funds. As regards the employers' overpayments, he observed that these would be returnable under a resulting trust. By contrast, the employees' contributions would go as bona vacantia to the Crown. Scott J. acknowledged that the fact that a party had received everything he had bargained for was not necessarily a decisive argument against a resulting trust. He felt that there could be no resulting trust in favour of the employees because he could devise no workable scheme to apportion the surplus contributions amongst different classes of employee. In *Air Jamaica v Charlton* (1999), however, Lord Millett did not approve of the approach in the Davis case and concluded that, as it was impossible to say that the members had received all that they had bargained for, a resulting trust of the surplus for employers and employees came into being. They were entitled in proportion to their respective contributions.

....

THE APPARENT GIFT CASES

Context

The second category in which the resulting trust traditionally makes an appearance is that of apparent gifts. This contains those resulting trusts that arise where there has been a contribution to the purchase price of property or a voluntary transfer of property into the name of another. Although both transactions may look like gifts, equity adopts a realistic interpretation of the parties' motivations and assumes, in the absence of contrary evidence, that they intended bargains not gifts. The imposition of the resulting trust is based on the rebuttable presumption that the transferor did not intend to benefit the transferee. This is sometimes referred to as the presumed intention resulting trust.

Purchase in the Name of Another

The basic idea is that, if X buys property in the name of Y, there is a presumption that Y holds the property on resulting trust for X: *Dyer v Dyer* (1788). There will also be a resulting trust where two people together provide the purchase price, but the property is held in the name of one of them only. For example, where the family home is conveyed only in the husband's name, but the wife had contributed to the purchase price, the husband will hold the legal estate on trust for himself and his wife. In *Sekhon v Alissa* (1989), a mother and daughter purchased a house together, but title was transferred only in the daughter's name. The mother was entitled to a beneficial interest by reason of a resulting trust in proportion to the amount of her contribution.

Legal title in joint names

In domestic cases where legal title is in joint names, the resulting trust approach has been jettisoned. Instead, as Baroness Hale put it in *Stack v Dowden* (2007), "the starting point where there is joint legal ownership is joint beneficial owner- ship". The onus now lies heavily with a party who wishes to show that the bene- ficial interests are divided otherwise than equally. This can be done by demonstrating a shared common intention of the parties to the effect that there should be ownership in different proportions. In determining this common inten- tion, the court may consider a wide range of issues. These could include, for example, financial and indirect contributions, advice received, discussions between the parties, reasons why the property was bought in joint names, the purposes for which the home was acquired, whether it was a home for the parties' children, how the parties arranged their finances and the nature of the parties' relationship. The court may also take into account how the circumstances have changed since the purchase. Indeed, Mrs Dowden was able to rebut the presump- tion by identifying a number of features that indicated a common intention that the beneficial interests were to be unequal. She had contributed far more to the acquisition of the property and the repayment of the mortgage than had her partner. Although they had lived together for 18 years, this was not a case where the parties pooled their resources for the common good.

Non-domestic settings

Two subsequent cases illustrate the circumstances in which the presumption of equal ownership arising from joint names may be rebutted:

- in *Adekunle v Ritchie* (2007) a mother and son bought a council house together under the right to buy legislation. The mother was a sitting tenant and had the benefit of a generous discount. She could not, however, fund the mortgage alone. The facts were, therefore, very different from that of the normal cohabiting couple. The primary purpose of the purchase was to provide a home for the mother and the parties' finances were kept separate. The judge awarded the son a one-third beneficial interest in the property;
- in *Laskar v Laskar* (2008), property was purchased by a mother and daughter as an investment. The presumption of equality did not apply as the property was bought for development or letting purposes and the resulting trust mechanism operated.

Limitations

The financial contribution must relate to the acquisition of the property. Except as to mortgage instalments, subsequent payments will not suffice. The payment must, moreover, be a direct contribution such as when one party pays either the deposit, part of the balance of the purchase price or the mortgage instalments. A "right to buy" discount under the Housing Act 1985 is also a direct contribution: *Springette v Defoe* (1992). Not all types of contribution will, however, count. For example, the following payments are insufficient:

- household expenses and running costs: *Burns v Burns* (1984);
- conveyancing costs and stamp duty: *Curley v Parkes* (2004);
- periodic payment of rent: *Savage v Dunningham* (1974), and
- improvements to the property except as between spouses and same-sex registered partnerships.

Quantum

The issue of quantum is, once the facts are established, a straightforward matter. In *Arogundade v Arogundade* (2005) a flat was purchased for £207,000. The claimant contributed £62,000 to the purchase price and, under resulting trust, obtained a 30 per cent share in the property. Put simply, you get back proportionately what you put in. The exact valuation of the share will normally be calculated as at the date of the eventual sale.

REBUTTING THE PRESUMPTION

The presumption of resulting trust is occasionally displaced by evidence of intention or a counter-presumption of equity (e.g. the *Stack v Dowden* presumption of equal ownership when the property is vested in joint names). Where there is evidence that money was provided by way of loan, for example, there can be no room for the presumption of resulting trust. Similarly, the presumption of a resulting trust will be displaced by evidence that the transferor or contributor intended to confer a gift. In *Walker v Walker* (1984), the public declaration by a father that he intended to give his newly wedded son the money to set up a home was sufficient to show an intention to benefit the son by way of gift.

Voluntary Transfer to Another
Personalty
On the voluntary transfer of personalty there will be a resulting trust unless there is either an express intention to make a gift or the presumption of advancement applies (see below). In *Re Vinogradoff* (1935), a grandmother made a lifetime transfer of £800 of War Loan shares to her young granddaughter. The transferor, however, continued to receive the dividends until her death. Subsequently, it was held that the granddaughter held the shares on resulting trust for the grandmother's estate. This case has been heavily criticised.

Land
As regards the voluntary transfer of land, s.60(3) of the **Law of Property Act 1925** provides that no resulting trust is presumed from the mere fact that the owner of a legal estate makes a gratuitous transfer of his estate into the hands of another. This is a word saving mechanism to ensure that it is not necessary to employ a particular formulation of words in order to render a voluntary conveyance to X effective. There is, however, nothing to prevent the resulting trust where there is other evidence indicative of the transferor's intention. In *Hodgson v Marks* (1971), Mrs Hodgson was persuaded to transfer her house to her lodger, Mr Evans, on the understanding that she would continue to be the beneficial owner. When he subsequently sold it to a purchaser, she was declared to have a beneficial interest under a resulting trust and, on the facts, this was binding on the purchaser.

Advancement

Which relationships?
Advancement might arise in the case of a voluntary conveyance from the transferor to:

- a wife: *Silver v Silver* (1958). This presumption is, however, easily rebutted in modern times. It is also gender biased because if the wife contributes all the money and the property is conveyed into the name of the husband, there is no presumption of a gift;
- a child: *Dyer v Dyer* (1788). The older cases indicate that there is no presumption of gift where a mother pays the purchase money and the property is in the name of the child: *Bennet v Bennet* (1879). This is because, in equity, there is no obligation on a mother to support her child, or
- someone with whom he/she stands in loco parentis (e.g. for example a stepchild, nephew, niece or a grandchild): *Re Paradise Motor Co Ltd* (1968). Although mothers are not caught by the previous head of advancement, it is thought that a widowed mother providing for her children would, at the least, fall within this category: *Re Grimes* (1937).

Rebutting the presumption of advancement
The presumption of advancement may be rebutted by evidence of a contrary intention. For example, in the case of land an express declaration of trust will, in the absence of fraud, be conclusive. There will be no room for the presumption of either advancement or a resulting trust: *Goodman v Gallant* (1986). In *Warrent v Gurney* (1944), the presumption of advancement was rebutted in circumstances where a father bought a house which was conveyed into the name of his daughter. The father retained the deeds. On his death, the daughter claimed unsuccessfully to be the beneficial owner of the house. The retention of the deeds, coupled with other evidence at the time of the purchase, rebutted the intention to make a gift.

Illegal purpose
Evidence of an illegal purpose cannot, however, be relied upon: *Tinsley v Milligan* (1993). The maxim "he who comes to equity must have clean hands"

applies here. The House of Lords emphasised that a person cannot rely on his own fraud or illegality to rebut the presumption of advancement. In *Tribe v Tribe* (1995), the issue was whether the transferor could rebut the presumption of advancement by adducing evidence of an illegal purpose that had not subsequently been carried into effect. It was held that when the planned illegal activity is never carried out, the transferor is not prevented from relying on evidence of his proposed activities to rebut the presumption of advancement. In *Lowson v Coombs* (1998), the rule was diluted further as, although an illegal purpose existed, it was not necessary to rely on that evidence in order to succeed. Hence, the illegal purpose was ignored. The illegality must, therefore, be invoked as evidence to justify the rebuttal of the presumption of advancement. For example, if a husband puts property into the name of a wife or a child in order to evade tax, he cannot then rely on this unlawful purpose in order to rebut the presumption of a gift: *Re Emery's Investment Trust* (1959).

Revision Checklist

You should now know and understand:

- **the default nature of the resulting trust;**
- **the various scenarios in which it may arise;**
- **how the beneficial interest under a resulting trust is calculated;**
- **the circumstances in which the presumption of a resulting trust may be rebutted.**

QUESTION AND ANSWER

The Question

In 2007, Jenny and Clare bought a house together in Keele Village. The property was registered in the sole name of Jenny. Clare discharged the legal fees and paid both the stamp duty and the removal expenses. In the past years, Clare has paid the utility bills, decorated the house and occasionally funded the mortgage repayments. Jenny and Clare never discussed the ownership of the house. Jenny and Clare have now ceased to be friends and Clare wishes to know what interest she has in the house.

Advise Clare. Would your advice differ if the property had been registered in their joint names?

This problem is about co-ownership and the means by which a non-legal owner can acquire an interest in another's property. This question is about resulting trusts and not constructive trusts. For the latter, there needs to be an express bargain (none here) or an implied bargain arising from the common intention of the parties (there is no common intention discernible here).

This type of case emphasises the inadequacy of resulting trust principles as regards those who share a home. A resulting trust is activated by financial contributions to the purchase price of the house. In addition, once activated Clare will only get back in proportion to her contribution: *Arogundade v Arogundade*. Looking at Clare's financial input, the problem is that the payment of conveyancing fees, stamp duty and removal costs do not count: *Curley v Parkes*. They are not directly connected to the acquisition payment for the house. Similarly paying the utility bills and undertaking decorating work concerns the running of the home and not the acquisition of the house: *Burns v Burns*. In any event such payments come too late to activate a purchase price resulting trust. Mortgage payments can, however, give rise to a resulting trust but only if Clare is under a legal obligation to the lender to make the payments: *Curley v Parkes*. Occasional and voluntary payments do not count for these purposes. Accordingly, Clare will not be able to claim an interest by virtue of a resulting trust.

If the property had been conveyed into joint names then different considerations apply. Following *Stack v Dowden*, the presumption is that Clare will share the house (their joint home) equally with Jenny (i.e. "Equity follows the Law"). It is then for Jenny to show that their common intention was not that they should share the property equally. As in *Stack*, it would appear that Jenny could do this easily. The parties seemingly did not pool their resources for their common good and Jenny's contribution to the purchase price far outweighs the value of the payments made by Clare: *Laskar v Laskar*.

Constructive Trusts

9

INTRODUCTION

Like the resulting trust, the constructive trust is a form of implied trust that arises by operation of law and not by the deliberate act of the parties. No formalities are required for its creation. It is a trust implied in a variety of circumstances where the defendant has knowledge of some factor that affects his conscience in respect of specific property. As Edmund Davies L.J. in *Carl Zeiss Stiftung v Herbert Smith & Co (No.2)* (1967) explained, "a constructive trust is a trust which is imposed by equity in order to satisfy the demands of justice and good conscience without reference to any express or presumed intention of the parties".

GENERAL PRINCIPLES

In *Westdeutsche Landesbank Girozentrale v Islington LBC* (1996), Lord Browne-Wilkinson laid down the following general principles:

- equity operates on the conscience of the owner of the legal interest;
- the legal owner cannot be a trustee until he is aware of the factors which are alleged to affect his conscience;
- there must be identifiable trust property. The only apparent exception to this rule is a constructive trust imposed on a person who dishonestly assists in a breach of trust who may come under fiduciary duties even if he does not receive identifiable trust property;
- from the date of the establishment of a constructive trust, the beneficiary has, in equity, a proprietary interest in the trust property. This is, enforceable in equity against any subsequent holder of the property (whether the original property or substituted property into which it can be traced) other than a purchaser for value of the legal interest without notice.

CATEGORIES

Unfortunately, there is little agreement as to how best to categorise the many examples of constructive trusts to be found in the case law. The following, however, provide useful illustrations:

- unauthorised fiduciary gains;
- liability imposed on strangers to the trust who knowingly receive trust property or dishonestly assist in cases of breach of trust;
- equitable response to wrongdoing or unconscionability; and
- enforcing the agreement between the parties.

Unauthorised Fiduciary Gains

A fiduciary is liable to his principal in respect of unauthorised gains obtained by reason of his fiduciary office. Fiduciaries include not only trustees, but also others who owe similar duties of loyalty and good faith to their principal, such as solicitors and company directors, partners and agents. Unauthorised gains may take a variety of forms, such as a secret profit (*William v Barton* (1927)), a bribe (*Att Gen for Hong Kong v Reid* (1994)) or the use of confidential information to make an unauthorised profit (*Boardman v Phipps* (1967)). Any profits made by exploiting trust property or the office of trustee are held by the trustee on constructive trust for the beneficiaries of the pre-existing trust.

Strangers to the Trust

This concerns a constructive trust that is imposed on a person who intermeddles or interferes with the trust so that he assumes the responsibilities of a trustee and faces consequent liability on that basis. This is grandly known as trustee-ship de son tort. The responsibilities of the trustee de son tort are the same as those of the express trustee. Similar liability extends to those who participate in the fraudulent conduct of the trustee. The personal liability of strangers to the trust now advances on two fronts.

Third parties who dishonestly assist in a breach of trust

A stranger to a trust can be liable in equity for assisting in a breach of trust, even though he has never received trust property. Where the third party dishonestly assists in the misapplication of trust property, he may be held personally liable in equity to restore the trust fund or to compensate the beneficiary for the loss occasioned to the trust fund. Although traditionally treated as invoking a constructive trust, in this type of case title to the property is never vested in the stranger. It is, therefore, technically incorrect to say that he is liable as a constructive trustee. Accessory liability is discussed further in Chapter 17.

Third parties who knowingly receive trust property in breach of trust

Liability to account on the basis of knowing receipt of trust property applies to strangers to the trust who receive trust property or its proceeds in the knowledge that the property has been misapplied or transferred in breach of trust. It is a pre-condition of liability that there has been a breach of trust. The requirements for liability for knowing receipt were listed by Hoffmann L.J. in *El Ajou v Dollar Land Holdings* (1994):

- a disposal of assets in breach of trust or fiduciary duty;
- the receipt by the defendant of assets which are traceable as representing the assets of the claimant, and
- knowledge on the part of the defendant that the assets he received are traceable to a breach of fiduciary duty. Note that, unlike liability for dishonest assistance, dishonesty is not a pre-requisite.

Unconscionability

A further context in which constructive trusts arise concerns general unconscionable behaviour, i.e. the prevention of "fraud". The courts have proved willing to apply constructive trust principles to a range of cases where the defendant acquires property belonging to another by unconscionable means.

Acquisition of property by killing

Understandably, the general principle is that a person should not benefit from the commission of a criminal act. A specific manifestation of this general principle is to be found in the forfeiture rule, i.e. a rule of public policy that precludes a person who has unlawfully killed another from acquiring a benefit as a consequence of the killing: in the *Estate of Crippen* (1911). Any property acquired by killing is to be held on constructive trust for the victim's estate. Some limited statutory relief is provided by the Forfeiture Act 1982. The Act applies to cases of unlawful killing other than murder and permits the court to grant relief from forfeiture where the justice of the case requires.

Absence of statutory formalities

Equity will not permit a statute to be used as an instrument of fraud. In *Bannister v Bannister* (1948), X conveyed legal title to two cottages to her brother-in-law for less than the market price. She was promised orally that she could reside in one of the cottages rent free for the remainder of her life. No mention of the promise was contained in the conveyance. It was not open to argue the absence of written evidence of the bargain between the parties.

Property acquired expressly subject to personal rights
Provided that his conscience is affected, a constructive trust can arise to bind the purchaser of property who agrees to take subject to a pre-existing interest. In *Binions v Evans* (1972), Mr Evans was permitted to live rent free in a cottage owned by his employer. On his death, he left a wife aged 73. Three years later the employer entered into an agreement with Mrs Evans that she could continue to live in the cottage for the remainder of her life as a tenant at will, rent free. In return, she agreed to keep the cottage in good repair. Subsequently, the cottage was sold to Mr and Mrs Binions expressly subject to the interest held by Mrs Evans. As a consequence, a reduced price was paid for the cottage. The Binions sought to evict Mrs Evans but this attempt failed. The Binions took the property subject to a constructive trust in favour of Mrs Evans. The payment of the lower price was significant.

Property acquired by joint venture
Equity will impose a constructive trust on property acquired by X in furtherance of an understanding with Y that, if Y refrains from entering the market, Y will be granted an interest in the property. In *Banner Homes Group Plc v Luff Developments Ltd (No.1)* (2000), the Court of Appeal outlined the necessary ingredients of liability:

- there must be a pre-acquisition understanding that the acquiring party will take steps to acquire the relevant property and that the non-acquiring party will obtain an interest in that property;
- there must be an advantage to the acquiring party gained, or a detriment to the non-acquiring party suffered, as a consequence of the understanding;
- it must be unconscionable to allow the acquiring party to retain the property for himself, in a manner inconsistent with the parties' agreement or understanding.

Enforcement of Agreements
The following illustrations mark out the role of the constructive trust in preventing a defendant from unconscionably resiling from an agreement entered into with the claimant. The selection of examples considered includes specifically enforceable contracts and mutual wills. Secret trusts provide another example, but these are discussed in Chapter 6. Constructive trusts of the family home are to be considered separately.

Specifically enforceable contracts for sale
Under a specifically enforceable contract for sale, the vendor becomes a constructive trustee of the property for the purchaser. This type of constructive

trust is based upon the maxim "equity looks on that as done that ought to be done". For example, once a contract for the sale of land has been made, the beneficial ownership of the property passes to the purchaser and the vendor is deemed to hold the legal estate on a constructive trust for him. Consequently, and subject to variation by agreement, it is for the purchaser to insure against damage to the property by fire or flood in the intervening time between contract and completion. If the vendor proceeds to sell to a third party, he is deemed to hold the purchase money on trust for the purchaser.

Mutual wills

Mutual wills arise where two or more parties enter into a binding agreement that they will execute wills in a mutual form on the understanding that the wills will be irrevocable. Typically, a husband and wife may enter into an agreement that each will execute a will whereby the survivor will inherit the property of the deceased spouse. On the death of the survivor, their pooled property will pass to nominated beneficiaries, usually, the children of the marriage. On the date of death of the first testator, a constructive trust comes into effect and it is no longer open to the surviving party to leave that property to an alternative beneficiary (e.g. to a new wife): *Re Haggar* (1930). By this means, equity intervenes in order to prevent the fraud that would arise if the survivor were able to take the benefit of the agreement without performing his obligations: *Goodman v Goodman* (1996).

....

AND THE FAMILY HOME?

Context

Unlike with divorce or the dissolution of a registered same sex partnership, on the breakdown of a relationship between cohabitants there is no overarching principle under which the parties' assets can be redistributed. Absent a formal declaration of trust, two legal mechanisms assume relevance, namely, the purchase money resulting trust (see Chapter 8) and the constructive trust. Due to the inflexibility of the resulting trust, the courts have, when possible, elected to rely upon constructive trust principles. This is attractive in that it offers scope to redistribute family assets according to judicial perceptions of what represents a fair outcome. In this context, there are two blends of constructive trust: the express bargain constructive trust and the implied bargain constructive trust: *Lloyds Bank v Rossett* (1990). Both operate to prevent a party from denying a common understanding as to beneficial entitlement when it would be unconscionable for this to occur.

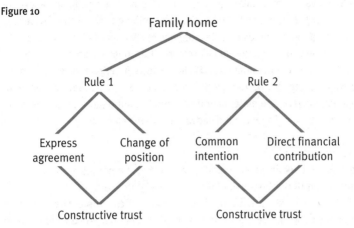

Figure 10

Family home

Rule 1　　　　Rule 2

Express agreement　　Change of position　　Common intention　　Direct financial contribution

Constructive trust　　　　Constructive trust

Express Bargain Constructive Trust

A constructive trust arises here in order to prevent one party resiling from an understanding as to beneficial entitlement in circumstances where it would be unconscionable to do so. This will occur only when there has been some discussion as to property rights between the parties and, consequently, some arrangement, agreement or understanding reached between them as to ownership. If no discussion occurs, as demonstrated in *Burns v Burns* (1984), there is no scope for a constructive trust under this head. The discussion will usually, but need not necessarily, occur prior to the acquisition of legal title.

KEY CASE

GRANT V EDWARDS (1986)

In *Grant v Edwards* (1986), George informed his partner, Linda, that the only reason the property was conveyed into his sole name was that her on-going divorce might be prejudiced if she was to be a joint legal owner. It was not the genuine desire of George that Linda become a beneficial owner. Nevertheless, she was led to believe that the property was to be theirs jointly. Hence, a constructive trust was imposed to ensure that she received the half-share in the house that George had led her to believe she would have.

Change of position

Once the court has found an express agreement, arrangement or understanding relating to the equitable ownership of the property, it is necessary to identify conduct by the claimant acting upon that intention. This is usually called detrimental reliance or change of position. The conduct relied upon can adopt a variety of guises and does not necessarily involve financial expenditure. In *Grant v Edwards* (1986) the claimant contributed to household expenses so that the defendant could meet the mortgage repayments. In *Eves v Eves* (1975), the claimant did not make any financial contribution, but did carry out substantial physical labour relating to internal and external decorating, gardening and general maintenance. She also performed the role of mother and housewife. The detriment must, however, be material and not merely emotional or psychological in nature. The court looks for a net disadvantage to the claimant.

Shares agreed

If the express bargain prescribes the shares that the parties are to take, the quantification of the beneficial interest is straightforward. In *Clough v Killey* (1996), there was an express bargain that the beneficial interest be shared on a 50:50 basis. Mrs Killey argued that a constructive trust arose which, due to the express agreement, gave her a 50 per cent interest. Subsequent to this arrangement, Mrs Killey had undeniably acted to her detriment by making the proceeds of her divorce settlement available to Mr Clough and undertaking work on the cottage. As to the extent of her share, Peter Gibson L.J. admitted, "it is only common sense that where the parties form a common intention as to specific shares they are to take, those shares prima facie are the shares to which the court will give effect".

Shares unagreed

Matters are more complicated when the express bargain does not prescribe the shares of each. In *Drake v Whipp* (1996), the court felt it necessary to look at all the circumstances, including contributions to the running of the home and family, to determine what constituted a fair share. This fair share approach has been adopted also in *Oxley v Hiscock* (2004) and *Stack v Dowden* (2006). This means that the court can look at direct financial contributions as well as indirect contributions such as payment of household expenses, contributions by way of labour and other actions of the claimant.

Implied Bargain Constructive Trust

A constructive trust arises here when there is no evidence of an express discussion having occurred between the parties. In this situation, the court looks in detail at the conduct of the parties with the prospect of presuming a common intention to share beneficial ownership.

Two key ingredients

First, the claimant must convince the court that there was a common intention to share the property beneficially. In the absence of a common intention, no common intention constructive trust will arise: *Lightfoot v Lightfoot-Brown* (2005). Following *Oxley v Hiscock* (2004), the task of finding a common intention has been simplified. Chadwick L.J. emphasised that direct contributions to the purchase price will be conduct from which such common intention can readily be inferred.

Secondly, the claimant must demonstrate that he changed his position on the basis of the unexpressed common intention. The change of position is localised only to direct financial contributions made to the initial and/or ongoing purchase of the property: *Gissing v Gissing* (1971). If direct contributions are found the courts will readily imply a constructive trust, whereas, if no such contributions are made, there can be no implied bargain constructive trust

Quantum

Although the making of direct financial contributions is necessary to buy entry into the co-ownership arena, it is important to appreciate that, once the constructive trust is invoked, the court can look beyond the direct contributions. In doing so it is able to divine a beneficial share which, on the facts of each case, accords with justice and good conscience. In *Midland Bank Plc v Cooke* (1995), the court undertook a survey of the whole course of dealing between the parties relevant to their ownership and occupation of the property and their sharing of its burdens and advantages. The contemporary tendency is, therefore, for the court to adopt a broad brush approach to the calculation of shares under the implied bargain: *Oxley v Hiscock* (2004).

Revision Checklist

You should now know and understand:

- **the general principles underpinning a constructive trust;**

- **the situations in which constructive trusts commonly arise;**

- **the operation of the constructive trust in the context of the family home;**

- **the distinctions between the express bargain and implied bargain types of constructive trust.**

QUESTION AND ANSWER

The Question

Tyson is the sole registered proprietor of a farmhouse situated in Yorkshire which he bought in 2005 with money from his savings. In 2007 he met and fell in love with Bruno and asked him to come and live with him. Tyson assured Bruno that "the farmhouse is as much yours as mine". Bruno agreed and gave up his job as a chef which provided a rent-free flat. The couple have now separated and Bruno is asserting a beneficial interest in the farmhouse.

Janice is the legal owner of a country cottage. Janice contributed 95 per cent of the initial purchase price with Deborah contributing the remaining 5 per cent. The couple never discussed the beneficial ownership of the cottage. In 2006, they adopted a child and Deborah gave up work to look after it. From that time, she undertook all the household duties and spent much of her free time building an extension to the cottage. Janice has now fallen in love with Abigail and seeks to sell the cottage. She has offered Deborah a settlement representing 5 per cent of the market value of the cottage.

Advise Bruno and Deborah.

Advice and the Answer

This problem question focuses primarily on the constructive trust as it operates in the family home.

As regards Bruno, there can be no resulting trust because there was no financial contribution to the purchase price of the property. The property was purchased long before Tyson met Bruno. Nevertheless, there was some express discussion of property rights and some agreement, arrangement or understanding ensued. As a result, Bruno changed his position by resigning from his post and giving up his rent free accommodation. This brings Bruno's claim squarely within Rule 1 of *Lloyds Bank v Rosset*. Hence, Bruno can establish the existence of a constructive trust. As to the calculation of his interest, in the normal course of events Bruno will be entitled to what was agreed: *Clough v Killey*. All turns upon the expression, "the farmhouse is as much yours as mine". This falls to be interpreted as giving Bruno a 50 per cent share in the property. By way of an alternative, it is possible that Bruno could succeed in a claim to proprietary estoppel: there is a certain representation, a change of position and it would be unconscionable to allow Tyson to renege on this informal agreement.

In relation to Deborah, she has made a financial contribution to the purchase price and, as shown in Chapter 8, she can claim a beneficial interest under a resulting trust. This will, however, only give her a 5 per cent interest. In the light of their relationship, she will undoubtedly want a greater share. Hence, Deborah will have to show the existence of a constructive trust. As there was no discussion of property rights, she cannot rely on Rule 1 of *Lloyds Bank v Rosset*. Instead, she will have to invoke Rule 2 and claim an implied bargain constructive trust. In order to do this, she must demonstrate that there was a common intention that she would have some interest in the property. This is easy to do as she has contributed directly to the purchase price. This direct contribution engages the implied trust, but does not limit her entitlement under it. The modern view, as promoted in *Oxley v Hiscock* and *Midland Bank v Cooke*, is that the court can look to all other factors (such as giving up work, child rearing and labouring) in order to divine a beneficial share that is fair and just on the facts. Although it is for the court to make this calculation, it is clear that Deborah will be entitled to far more than a 5 per cent share.

Non-charitable Purpose Trusts

INTRODUCTION

This Chapter focuses upon the validity of trusts designed to further non-charitable purposes (sometimes called "Trusts of Imperfect Obligation"). The general rule is that non-charitable purpose trusts are void: *Re Astor's Settlement Trusts* (1952). By their very nature their object is a purpose and they lack a beneficiary to enforce the trust. This chapter will examine:

* the beneficiary principle;
* the permitted historical exceptions to the beneficiary principle;
* the dividing line between trusts for persons and trusts for purposes; and
* property holding by unincorporated associations.

THE BENEFICIARY PRINCIPLE

For a trust to be valid it must have a human beneficiary by whom the trust can be enforced: *Morice v Bishop of Durham* (1804). As mentioned, the general rule is that private purpose trusts are void. This has become known as the beneficiary principle. The courts have struck down a variety of non-charitable purpose trusts such as:

* "the preservation of the independence of newspapers": *Re Astor's Settlement Trusts* (1952);
* "the provision of some useful monument to myself": *Re Endacott* (1960), and
* a trust to promote a new 40-letter alphabet: *Re Shaw* (1957).

Charitable Trusts

The beneficiary principle is limited to private trusts. Where the purpose of the trust is charitable the absence of a human beneficiary is not fatal. A charitable trust can, where necessary, be enforced by the Attorney General and the Charity Commission (see Chapter 11).

The operation of the rule against perpetuities has relevance in relation to pure purpose trusts and gifts for unincorporated associations. There are two major aspects to the rule against perpetuities.

The rule against remoteness of future vesting, which deals with the maximum length of time for which the vesting of future interests in the beneficiaries can be postponed. This is concerned with commencement of interests. As regards unincorporated associations, care as to be taken if the funds are to benefit future (as well as present) members. In such an instance, the gift must be structured so as to end within the perpetuity period.

The rule against inalienability. This rule seeks to ensure that property is not tied up in a trust for longer than an acceptable perpetuity period or, indeed, for an indefinite period. This second aspect plays an important role in the context of trusts for non-charitable purposes. For example, where a testator seeks to cater for the maintenance of a monument or tomb, it is important that a valid perpetuity period is selected.

Anomalous Exceptions

There are some odd cases where a trust has been upheld even though it clearly advances a private purpose. If a pure purpose trust is upheld, it is essential that the trustee must give an undertaking to perform the trust. If the funds are misapplied by the trustee, those entitled to the residuary estate can complain to the court. These exceptional cases were decided before *Re Astor* (1952) and, based upon a dubious foundation, are unlikely to be followed in modern times. Indeed, in *Re Endacott* (1960), these exceptions were described as "troublesome, anomalous and aberrant."

Care of specific animals

In *Pettingall v Pettingall* (1842), a trust of £50 to look after the testator's favourite mare for 50 years was upheld. In *Re Dean* (1889), a gift of £750 per annum to maintain the testator's horses, ponies and hounds "if they should so long live" was held to be valid.

Monuments and graves

In *Pirbright v Salwey* (1896), £800 was given to the rector of the parish to use the income for the upkeep of a grave. This case was followed in *Re Hooper* (1932) which concerned the upkeep of family tombs and monuments. Similarly, in *Mussett v Bingle* (1876), £300 left to erect a monument to the first husband of the testator's wife was valid. Maintenance of private graves is now possible for 99 years under s.1 of the Parish Councils and Burial Authorities (Miscellaneous Provisions) Act 1970.

Trusts for private masses

In *Bourne v Keane* (1919), a trust for the saying of private masses for an individual was held valid by the House of Lords. Note that masses open to the public are categorised as charitable: *Re Hetherington* (1989).

Promotion and furtherance of foxhunting

In *Re Thompson* (1934), a trust to promote these purposes was upheld on the facts. Not surprisingly, the decision has never been followed. Here the trustee was prepared to act in accordance with the settlor's desires.

Figure 11

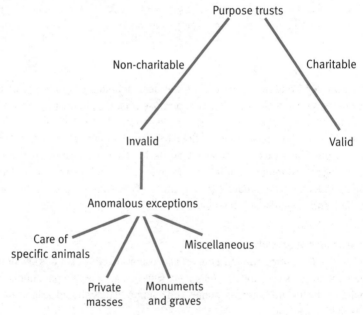

TRUSTS FOR PERSONS OR FOR PURPOSES?

A possible area of confusion involves legitimate private trusts for individuals that are expressed in the form of a purpose or limited by a purpose.

RE SANDERSON'S TRUST (1857), RE BOWES (1896) AND RE DENLEY'S TRUST DEED (1969)

- In *Re Sanderson's Trust* (1857), the testator's property was left upon trust "to pay or apply the whole or any part of" towards the maintenance, attendance and comfort of his brother. This was not a purpose trust as the purpose in this case provided merely the means to calculate the amount of his beneficial share.
- In *Re Bowes* (1896), £5000 was left on trust to estate owners for the purpose of planting trees on the estate for shelter. The land would have benefited from £800 worth of trees, any further planting working to the disadvantage of the beneficiaries. Accordingly, it was held that the owners of the estate were absolutely entitled to the £5,000. Again, the purpose merely expressed the motive of the gift.
- In *Re Denley's Trust Deed* (1969), a trust to provide a recreation ground for the benefit of employees of a company was viewed as a valid trust because the employees were a class of beneficiaries with sufficient standing to enforce the trust. It was not a pure purpose trust. Goff J. explained, "when, then, the trust though expressed as a purpose, is directly or indirectly for the benefit of an individual or individuals, it seems to me that it is in general outside the mischief of the beneficiary principle".

UNINCORPORATED ASSOCIATIONS

DEFINITION CHECKPOINT

Many groups and societies such as sports and social clubs are committed to the pursuit of non-charitable purposes. An unincorporated association is a body or group of individuals that has not been incorporated as a company. Unlike companies, unincorporated bodies or groups do not have legal personality and are, therefore, unable to hold property in their own name.

In *Conservative & Unionist Central Office v Burrell* (1982), the Court of Appeal identified five characteristics of an unincorporated association:

- two or more persons;
- a non-business common purpose;
- the undertaking of mutual duties and mutual obligations between members;
- a body of governing rules and
- a fluctuating body of members.

Three possibilities

Following *Neville Estates v Madden* (1962), a gift to an unincorporated association is likely to be construed in one of three ways.

A gift to present members of the association at the date of the gift

The members could, if they wanted, divide the property between themselves, each taking a share. This was the construction put upon a gift in *Cocks v Manners* (1871) where a testator left a share of his residue to the Dominican Convent at Carisbrooke "payable to the superior for the time being".

A gift on trust for the purposes of the association

On this construction the gift would fail for lack of a human beneficiary. In *Leahy v Att Gen (New South Wales)* (1959), a gift of a sheep station for "such order of nuns of the Catholic Church or the Christian brothers as my trustees shall select" was held not to be a gift for individual members of the order. It was expressed to be for the benefit of religious orders rather than for specified individuals. The gift was not, moreover, charitable under the head of advancement of religion because it was a purely contemplative order of nuns. Accordingly, the gift failed because there were no individual beneficiaries.

A gift to the members subject to their respective contractual rights and liabilities

This is known as the contract holding theory. In such a case, the property will accrue to the others on the death or resignation of a member, even though such members include persons who became members after the gift took effect. This was, indeed, the preferred option in *Neville Estates v Madden* (1962). It heralded an approach favoured also in *Re Lipinski's Will Trust* (1976), where the testator left part of his residuary estate to the Hull Judeans (Maccabi) Association "to be used solely in the work of constructing the new buildings for the association and for improvements to the said building". It was held that the gift was not a pure purpose trust and was, instead, for the benefit of ascertainable beneficiaries. The trust was valid because the members of the association had the power to alter the purpose for which the money could be used and could divide the money between themselves.

A number of points are now clear:

- The contract holding theory has emerged as the preferred and most convenient construction of property holding by unincorporated associations: *Re Horley Town Football Club* (2006).
- If the members of the association have no control over the funds the trust will fail. In *Re Grants Will Trusts* (1980), there was a trust for the

purposes of the Chertsey Labour Party Headquarters. There the members did not control the property nor could they change their constitution to enable them to do so. The fact that third parties have voting rights and can influence rule changes does not prevent the contract holding theory applying: *Re Horley Town Football Club* (2006).

- On the dissolution of an unincorporated association, the funds are distributed to reflect how the members held the property in the first place in accordance with their contract: *Re Bucks Constabulary Fund (No.2)* (1979). There was in that case an equal distribution of the funds between the surviving members (to the exclusion of former members) in line with the contract holding theory. This rule gives way when the society is moribund (i.e. has no more than one member left) as then the funds will go bona vacantia to the Crown.

Revision Checklist

You should now know and understand:

- **the problems associated with non-charitable purposes trusts;**

- **the beneficiary principle and the exceptions to it;**

- **the distinction between a trust for persons or a trust for purposes;**

- **how unincorporated associations hold property (in conjunction with Chapter 8);**

- **the consequences following on from the dissolution of an unincorporated association.**

QUESTION AND ANSWER

The Question

Critically examine the construction of gifts to unincorporated associations.

A good answer to this question requires an understanding of the beneficiary principle, i.e. that a trust must be for the benefit of ascertainable individuals and that, accordingly, it is not possible to create a private purpose trust. Subject to a limited number of historical exceptions, it is simply not possible to set up a valid trust for purposes. This straightforward conclusion, that private purpose trusts are void for want of a beneficiary, was tested in *Re Denley*, where a gift of property to employees for the purpose of a recreation ground was upheld on the basis that it did not offend the rule against perpetuities and because it served an ascertainable class of "beneficiaries" with sufficient standing to enforce the trust.

Gifts to unincorporated associations assume relevance in this context because an unincorporated association is a body of individuals bound together to pursue common purposes (*Burrell*). It is common, therefore, for individuals to seek to further particular purposes by way of gifts to such associations. There are two important issues that must be addressed in your answer: firstly, the nature of property holding by such associations and the construction of gifts to such associations to further specific purposes.

The most common construction of property holding by unincorporated associations is the contract holding theory (*Neville Estates v Madden*) i.e. that members hold property subject to their respective contractual rights and liabilities towards one another. Gifts construed in this way are treated in accordance with the rules of the association as an accretion to the funds of the association (*Re Recher's WT*), with funds held by the treasurer to be disbursed in accordance with the contractual rules. Crucially, within this construction, the members of the association must retain control over property holding (*Re Grant's WT*), be free to alter its purposes (*Re Lipinski's WT*) and, ultimately, to dissolve the association and distribute the property amongst themselves (*Re Bucks Constabulary (No.2)*).

Although the contract holding theory is the preferred construction, it remains possible to make an outright gift to present members (*Cocks v Manners*), or to create a trust for the present members as joint tenants or tenants in common. Gifts on trust for present and future members create most difficulty, as these must comply with the perpetuity rules. Perhaps, where perpetuity is not a concern, the principle in *Re Denley* may save a gift, construed for the benefit of present and future members, who may be deemed to have sufficient standing to enforce the trust.

Charitable Trusts

11

INTRODUCTION

Charitable trusts are public trusts. They are usually designed to promote a purpose that is beneficial to society. A charitable trust may also be framed so as to benefit a particular charitable organisation (which can be a company or an unincorporated association). As will be shown, the attraction of achieving charitable status is that it brings with it a variety of fiscal and legal privileges. In order to be charitable a trust must satisfy three requirements: it must be inherently charitable (i.e. listed in s.2(2) of the Charities Act 2006, analogous to something listed or something that was charitable prior to the Act), for the public benefit and exclusively charitable.

THE 13 HEADS OF CHARITY

Section 2(2)(a)–(m) of the **Charities Act 2006** contains a new and broad list of charitable purposes:

(a) the prevention or relief of **poverty**;

(b) the advancement of **education**;

(c) the advancement of **religion**;

(d) the advancement of **health or the saving of lives**. This includes the prevention of or relief of sickness, disease or human suffering;

(e) the advancement of **citizenship or community development**. This includes rural or urban regeneration and the promotion of civic responsibility, volunteering, the voluntary sector or the effectiveness or efficiency of charities;

(f) the advancement of the **arts, culture, heritage or science**;

(g) the advancement of **amateur sport**. For these purposes sport means sport or games which promote health by involving physical or mental skill or exertion;

(h) the advancement of **human rights, conflict resolution or reconciliation or the promotion of religious or racial harmony or equality and diversity**;

(i) the advancement of **environmental protection or improvement**;

(j) the relief of those in need, by reason of youth, age, ill-health, disability, financial hardship or other disadvantage. This includes relief given by the provision of accommodation or care to such persons;
(k) the advancement of animal welfare;
(l) the promotion of the efficiency of the armed forces of the Crown or the efficiency of the police, fire and rescue services or ambulance services;
(m) other purposes currently recognised as charitable and any new charitable purposes which are similar to another charitable purpose.

PUBLIC BENEFIT

This entails that it must be of benefit to the public at large or a sufficient section thereof: s.2(1)(b) of the 2006 Act. Section 3 explains that in determining whether there is a public benefit, it is not to be presumed that a purpose of a particular description is automatically for the public benefit. The Charity Commission publishes guidance from time to time providing its interpretation of what constitutes the public benefit. A public benefit test is applied, but the nature of the test varies according to which head of charity is being considered.

EXCLUSIVELY CHARITABLE?

This entails that the property must be capable of dedication to charitable purposes only: s.1(1)(a) of the 2006 Act. Accordingly, where a gift is given for a number of specific purposes it will not be a valid charitable trust unless all the purposes are charitable.

KEY CASES

MORICE V BISHOP OF DURHAM (1805), RE WARD (1941), RE EADES (1920), RE BEST (1904), SALUSBURY V DENTON (1857) AND RE COXEN (1948)

- In *Morice v Bishop of Durham* (1805), a gift for "benevolent purposes" was held not to be exclusively charitable because some benevolent purposes are not charitable at law.
- The word "or", imports an alternative and is said to be disjunctive: *Re Ward* (1941). Phrases such as "charitable or benevolent", "charitable or deserving" and so on have been held to lack the necessary exclusivity.

- In *Re Eades* (1920), references were made to "religious, charitable and philanthropic" purposes. The use of the **comma** after "religious" indicated that each class was separate and disjunctive and, therefore, the trust was not exclusively charitable.
- In *Re Best* (1904), "charitable and benevolent" was held to be exclusively charitable. Although "benevolent" is open to a non-charitable meaning, the words were linked to an overt charitable purpose by use of the word **"and"**.
- If a trustee is directed to divide property between charitable and non-charitable objects the trust will not wholly fail. In default of apportionment, the court may divide the fund equally and the trust will be valid as to the charitable half: *Salusbury v Denton* (1857).
- In *Re Coxen* (1948), the fact that a testator directed that £100 of a charitable fund of £200,000 could be used for a dinner for the trustees did not stop the trust from being exclusively charitable. The non-charitable aspect was merely ancillary to the main charitable purpose.

Figure 12: Is it Charitable?

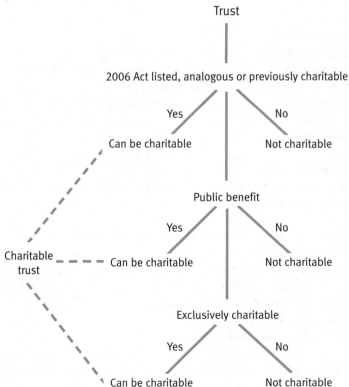

Trust

2006 Act listed, analogous or previously charitable

Yes — Can be charitable
No — Not charitable

Public benefit

Yes — Can be charitable
No — Not charitable

Exclusively charitable

Yes — Can be charitable
No — Not charitable

Charitable trust

ADVANTAGES OF CHARITABLE STATUS

Enforceability

Charitable trusts do not require ascertainable beneficiaries to enforce them. They are enforceable by the Attorney General. The Charity Commission has administrative responsibilities and can exercise powers of enforcement with the consent of the Attorney General.

Certainty

Charitable trusts differ from private trusts in that the objects of a charitable trust need not be certain. Provided the objects are wholly and exclusively charitable, the courts or the Charity Commission can remedy any vagueness by preparing a scheme for the application of funds. In *Moggridge v Thackwell* (1803), the testatrix left property to her trustee to divide, as he saw fit, between charities. The trustee predeceased the testatrix, but the courts upheld the trust and devised a scheme as to how the money was to be distributed. The cy-près doctrine, which allows for the dedication of trust property to purposes as near as possible to those originally selected, is considered in Chapter 12.

Perpetuity

A charity is not subject to the rule against alienability that applies to pure purpose trusts. Accordingly, capital can be dedicated indefinitely to, for example, the relief of poverty or the advancement of religion. In addition, although a gift to charity must vest within the perpetuity period, a gift over from one charity to another can occur outside the perpetuity period: *Christ's Hospital v Grainger* (1849).

Tax Advantages

The main advantage of charitable status is the privileged tax position that it attracts. For example:

- relief from income tax on investment income applicable to exclusively charitable purposes;
- exemption from tax on trading income where either the trade is exercised in the course of carrying out the primary charitable purposes of the charity, or the work in connection with the trade is mainly carried out by the beneficiaries of the charity;
- exemptions from capital gains tax;
- a claim to at least 80 per cent relief from the payment of non-domestic rates for premises wholly or mainly used for charitable purposes; and
- exemptions from payment of stamp duty on conveyances.

THE KEY HEADS OF CHARITY

Under the **2006 Act**, the main heads of charity will remain poverty (s.2(2)(a)); the advancement of education (s.2(2)(b)) and the advancement of religion (s.2(2)(c)). The remaining 10 heads may, for convenience, still be grouped together as "other charitable purposes". It is, however, possible for a purpose to fall within more than one of the headings.

RELIEF OF POVERTY

Meaning
Poverty is not limited to destitution and, in *Re Coulthurst* (1951), was equated with persons who have to "go short". There, a gift to be applied for widows and orphaned children of deceased employees of a particular bank was upheld as charitable. In *Garfield Poverty Trust* (1995), it was held that those who could not afford to take on a mortgage could be classified as being "poor" and, hence, the provision of interest free loans to buy houses was charitable. Gifts have been upheld even when the poorest have been excluded. In *Re De Carteret* (1933), an annuity of £40 to widows and spinsters, whose annual income would otherwise be not less than £8 and no more than £120, was upheld.

Need
It is not necessary that the words "poverty" or "poor" be employed. For example, in *Re Scarisbrick* (1951) the expression "in needy circumstances" indicated poverty. Similarly, in *Re Gardom* (1914) the expression "of limited means" was sufficient. In *Re Cohen* (1919), however, the term "deserving" did not connote a sufficient need and was not charitable. Poverty may also be inferred from the nature of the gift. In *Biscoe v Jackson* (1887) the provision of a soup kitchen qualified under the head of poverty. In *Re Gosling* (1900), the provision of a superannuation fund for "pensioning off old worn out clerks" was viewed as being implicitly for the relief of poverty. A borderline example is *Re Niyazi* (1978) where the construction of a working men's hostel in Cyprus was held to be charitable.

Public Benefit?
It is arguable that there is no public benefit test whatsoever that applies to poverty. If such a test exists, however, it is hardly demanding. This leniency is explained on the basis that the relief of poverty is so altruistic that a public benefit element can be necessarily inferred. Accordingly, a trust for a testator's poor relations is charitable: *Isaac v Defriez* (1754). Similarly, in *Re Gosling* (1900) poor employees were permitted to benefit. The **Charities Act** requires charities seeking registration to demonstrate that they deliver a public benefit. It still

remains necessary to distinguish between a private trust and a public (i.e. charitable) trust. In *Re Scarisbrick* (1951), the distinction was drawn between a trust to benefit named poor relations (a private trust) and a trust to benefit unnamed poor relations (a public trust). The Court of Appeal made clear also that a trust for the relief of poverty would not be charitable if the poor persons to benefit were members of a narrow class of close family. In *Re Segelman* (1996), a gift to poor and needy members of a class of six named relatives and their descendants (who totalled 26 persons on the testator's death) was upheld. Chadwick J. acknowledged that the gift could not be charitable if it was in essence a gift to the individual members of the class. In his view, however, the gift was not of that character. The selection of named beneficiaries focused on need and not mere closeness of relationship. This is a borderline case.

Exclusively Charitable?

It is also necessary that a trust to relieve poverty is exclusively charitable. A trust will not be for the relief of poverty if it can benefit the rich as well as the poor. In *Re Gwyon* (1930), a trust to establish a clothing foundation to provide clothing to boys in Farnham floundered because it failed to exclude more affluent children. The case demonstrates that benefits must be restricted to the poor.

ADVANCEMENT OF EDUCATION

Meaning

Education is not restricted to formal education in educational institutions such as schools and universities. It is, however, necessary that there is some element of instruction or improvement. Although research can clearly fall under the umbrella of education, there must be more than simply an accumulation of knowledge.

Research

- In *Re Shaw* (1957), the settlor directed his trustees to use his residuary estate for a number of specified purposes. These included the devising of a new 40-letter alphabet and the translation of some of plays into that new alphabet. It was held not to be charitable because there was "no element of teaching or education".
- In *Re Hopkin's Will Trust* (1965) the testatrix bequeathed some of her residuary estate to the Francis Bacon Society. This was to be applied towards discovering evidence of Bacon's authorship of plays usually accredited to Shakespeare. Upholding the charitable nature of this trust, Wilberforce J. held that research can be regarded as charitable when it is

worthwhile (unlike in *Re Shaw*) and will lead to something which will pass into the store of educational material.

Public services
Education extends to the provision of educational public services and is wide enough to include forms of worthwhile instruction These activities also fall within a separate head of charity as listed in s.2(2)(f) of the **Charities Act 2006**. For example, the provision of botanical gardens, museums, libraries and choirs. In *Incorporated Council of Law Reporting v Att Gen* (1972) the preparation of law reports was held to be charitable. In *Re Delius* (1957), the wife of the composer Delius gave her residuary estate for the advancement of her late husband's work. This was held to be charitable because the trust was to spread knowledge and appreciation of Delius' work throughout the world. In *Re Pinion* (1965), however, an artist left his studio and its contents to trustees to enable it to be used as a museum to display his collection of works. Harman L.J. admitted, "I can see of no useful object to be served in foisting upon the public this mass of junk. It has neither public utility nor educational value". It was held not to be charitable.

Sport
Trusts to advance sports within an educational institution may be charitable also under the head of education. In *Re Mariette* (1915), there was a valid charitable trust to provide squash courts at Aldenham School and a prize for athletics. Nevertheless, the sporting facilities do not necessarily have to be at a particular school. In *IRC v McMullen* (1981), a trust to provide facilities for soccer at schools and universities in the United Kingdom was held to assist the physical education and development of the young. Under the **Charities Act 2006**, the promotion of amateur sport is itself a separate head of charity; s.2(2)(g).

Public Benefit?
There must be a genuine public benefit in educational trusts. The law is anxious that educational trusts should not be used as a tax avoidance measure to provide education for the wealthy at the expense of the taxpayer. Similarly, the law will not allow employers to gain commercial advantage by setting up educational trusts for the children of their employees. Hence, in *Re Compton* (1945) a trust providing for the education of the descendants of three named persons was not a valid charitable trust. As the beneficiaries were defined by reference to a personal relationship, the trust lacked any public element.

Blood and contract rule
In *Oppenheim v Tobacco Securities Trust Co Ltd* (1951), the House of Lords approved a test that has become known as "the blood and contract rule" or

"the personal nexus test". In that case, money was given to provide education for the children of employees of the British American Tobacco Corporation and its subsidiaries. The number of employees exceeded 110,000. It was held that, even with these large numbers, the personal nexus between the employers and employees meant that there was not a sufficient public benefit. Lord MacDermott, however, dissented. He considered that the public benefit question should be one of degree depending on the facts of the particular case. Attempts are sometimes made to side-step the blood and contract rule.

- In *Re Koettgen's Will Trust* (1954), a trust was established to further the education of British born persons, with a direction that preference be given to employees of a particular company in respect of 75 per cent of fund. The trust was held to be primarily for the public, a mere preference being given to employee's families. This decision is open to question and appears to undermine the policy underlying the blood and contract rule.
- In *IRC v Educational Grants Association Ltd* (1967), however, a trust to advance education was set up by the Metal Box Company. The evidence showed that over 80 per cent of the payments made went towards the education of children connected to the company. The trust was held not to be charitable.

Exclusively Charitable?

In *Southwood v Att Gen* (2000) a project on demilitarisation based at Bradford University failed because the political dimension of the trust prevented it being exclusively educational in nature. It was political propaganda and, therefore, not in the public interest. Similarly, in *Re Hopkinson* (1949) a trust to educate the public in the aims of a political party (Labour) could not be charitable because it amounted to political propaganda and was not exclusively educational. However, in, *Att Gen v Ross* (1986), a gift to London Polytechnic Students Union was charitable even though it had ancillary non-charitable purposes (e.g. providing shops and a bar).

ADVANCEMENT OF RELIGION

Meaning

The law draws no distinction between one religion and another and adopts the view that any religion is better than none: *Neville Estates v Madden* (1962). The courts feel ill equipped to make value judgments on the inherent benefit of particular religious beliefs: *Holmes v Att Gen* (1981). For example, in *Thornton v Howe* (1862) a trust for the publication of the works of Joanna Southcote was held to be charitable. She claimed that she had been impregnated by the

Holy Ghost and would give birth to the second Messiah. Charitable status will be refused to any religion that is deemed to be subversive of morality, contrary to the public interest or adverse to the very foundations of all religion. The worship of Satan or the promotion of black magic cannot be charitable. Paganism and trusts for the promotion of paganism have also not been viewed with favour.

A spiritual connection?
For a religion to exist prior to the **2006 Act** there had to be some belief in the existence of some Supreme Being and the worship of that being. Section 2(3)(a) of the **2006 Act** now provides that religion includes one which involves belief in more than one god and a religion which does not believe in a god at all. This represents a move to overcome doubt that Buddhism is a religion for charitable purposes. In *Re South Place Ethical Society* (1980), the society existed to cultivate "rational religious sentiment". It was, however, an agnostic society interested in ethical and rational principles and charitable status was denied. Dillon J. explained, "Religion is concerned with man's relations with God and ethics are concerned with man's relations with man". In *Power, Praise and Healing Mission* (1976), a trust for the advancement of religion by means including exorcism was granted charitable status. Gifts to repair a church, to provide a stained glass window, to finance the purchase of an organ and to train clergy, for example, will fall within this head of charity.

Public Benefit?
The religion must benefit a sufficient section of the community. This rule is illustrated by *Gilmour v Coates* (1949) where property was left on trust for a Carmelite convent. The Carmelites are a contemplative order who do not venture outside the convent walls. It was concluded that prayer and spiritual belief alone were of no tangible benefit to the public. In contrast, the *Society of the Precious Blood* (1995) concerned Anglican nuns and this was held to be charitable. These nuns were not cut off from the outside world. They worked in the community and provided classes and talks. Unlike *Gilmour*, this obviously had a public benefit.

Examples
The provision of a retreat house may be charitable if it is open to the public: *Neville Estates v Madden* (1962). A gift for private masses is not charitable. A gift for masses for the dead has, however, been held to have sufficient public benefit when the mass is part of a public ritual: *Re Hetherington* (1990). Similarly, a gift to maintain an individual tomb lacks public benefit, but the maintenance of all the tombs in a churchyard is charitable: *Thompson v Pritcher* (1815).

Exclusively Charitable?

A charitable purpose might be linked with another purpose and it is then necessary to look at wording used. If the gift is limited to, for example, the office of a priest or vicar, it will be deemed to be exclusively charitable: *Re Rumball* (1956) (a bishop). Similarly, in *Re Simson* (1946) a gift to a vicar "for his work in the parish" was upheld as a gift to that person limited to purposes defined by his office. In *Farley v Westminster Bank* (1939), however, a gift to a vicar "for parish work" was not viewed as being a gift for his work as a vicar in the parish. As it was not directly linked to his office as vicar, it embraced non-charitable purposes.

OTHER CHARITABLE PURPOSES

Meaning of Other Purposes

This description represents a ragbag of worthy causes that have been recognised as charitable. The **Charities Act 2006** lists 10 categories which fall within this head (see above s.2(2)(d)-(m)). Not every purpose beneficial to the community will, however, be classified as charitable and the list in s.2(2) is not exhaustive. If not listed in the **2006 Act**, the purpose must fall within the spirit and intendment of the **2006 Act** or have been recognised as charitable under the previous law: s.2(4). In *Council of Law Reporting for England and Wales v Att Gen* (1972), Russell L.J. said that if the purpose cannot be viewed as anything other than being beneficial to the community, it should be charitable unless there is any reason for holding it not to be so.

- a gift for a Fire Brigade: (*Re Wokingham Fire Brigade Trusts* (1951); see now s.2(2)(l) of the **2006 Act**);
- gifts for the increased efficiency or morale of the army: (*Re Good* (1905); see now s.2(2)(l) of the **2006 Act**);
- gifts for the promotion of industry, commerce and art: (*Crystal Palace Trustees v Minister of Town & Country Planning* (1950)) see now s.2(2)(e)(f) of the 2006 Act;
- trusts for the promotion of sport in the army: *Re Gray* (1925) see now s.2(2)(g), (l) of the **2006 Act**;
- trusts to promote physical wellbeing: e.g. to provide guide dogs, to build hospitals, to protect vulnerable children, to prevent alcoholism and drug abuse and to offer family planning advice (see now s.2(2)(j) of the **2006 Act**);
- trusts for the protection of animals generally will be upheld if they promote and encourage human kindness: *Re Wedgewood* (1915); see now s.2(2)(k) of the 2006 Act. In *Re Grove-Grady* (1929), however, a sanctuary for

animals or birds to keep them safe from molestation by man was not a charitable purpose. The court could discern no benefit in stopping people becoming involved with animals.

Public Benefit?
In many of the examples of gifts considered to fall under this fourth head of charity, the gift is for the potential benefit of the whole public. It does not matter that only a limited number of people will actually take advantage of it. For example, the provision of a bridge is a charitable purpose provided that it is available for everyone to use. It does not lose charitable status simply because only a few people decide to use it. It will not be charitable, however, if the use of the bridge is confined to a selected number of persons, no matter how large that number is. This is traditionally called the class within a class rule.

In *IRC v Baddeley* (1955), a controversy arose over a trust for the promotion of the religious, social and physical well being of the Methodists of West Ham and Leyton. It failed, in part, because social purposes were not charitable. This decision led to the passing of the Recreational Charities Act 1958 (as amended) which provides that it is charitable to provide, or assist in the provision of facilities for recreation or other leisure-time occupation, if the facilities are provided in the interests of social welfare. This requires that the facilities be provided with the object of improving the conditions of life for the persons for whom the facilities are primarily intended. In addition, either the persons have need of these facilities by reason of youth, age, infirmity or disablement, poverty or social and economic circumstances; or the facilities are to be available to the members of the public at large or to male or female members of the public at large. The Act covers facilities at village halls, community centres and women's institutes as well as the provision and maintenance of grounds and buildings to be used for purposes of recreation and leisure. These charitable purposes are expressly preserved by s.2(4)(a) of the **2006 Act**.

Social and Recreational Purposes Class within a class rule
In *IRC v Baddeley* (1955), a trust was established to promote the moral, social and physical wellbeing of persons resident in West Ham who were members of the Methodist Church. The House of Lords held that this was not charitable under the fourth head. The distinction was drawn between a benefit that is extended to the whole community (even though advantageous only to a few) and relief accorded to a selected few out of a larger number. Viscount Simmonds explained, "the beneficiaries are a class within a class; they are those of the inhabitants of a particular area who are members of a particular church". Unless

excluded by s.2, the class within a class rule will continue to operate in relation to the 'other purposes' group of character heads.

Political trusts

Political trusts are never charitable. The traditional reasoning is that the court has no means of judging whether a proposed change in the law will or will not be for the public benefit: *Bowman v Secular Society* (1917). As demonstrated in *McGovern v Att Gen* (1982), if there is an aim to change the law, to promote a particular political party or theory or to seek to change governmental policy either here or abroad it is not charitable. For example, charities dealing with poverty are not allowed to campaign against the social and economic causes of poverty. In *National Anti-Vivisection Society v IRC* (1948), money was given to further the cause of anti-vivisection. The court held that the moral benefit resulting to mankind was outweighed by the detriment that would be suffered by medical research if experiments were not allowed on live animals. The case failed also because it had a political element in that it sought to promote legislation to change the law that allowed vivisection.

Exclusively Charitable?

As with the other heads of charity, the gift must be exclusively charitable. In *McGovern v Att Gen* (1982), Amnesty International sought charitable status. Although the social benefits of Amnesty's work are readily apparent and look to be caught by s.2(2)(h) of the **2006 Act** (e.g. promotion of human rights, assisting prisoners of conscience and seeking the abolition of torture and inhumane punishment), it was not exclusively charitable. Its major aims included changing the law and influencing the policies of governments around the world. It was tainted with a political character. It is, therefore, common for such organisations to separate their charitable projects from their non-charitable work.

Revision Checklist

You should now know and understand:

- **the advantages of charitable status;**
- **the 13 statutory heads of charity;**
- **the different public benefit tests which operate;**
- **the requirement that the purpose be exclusively charitable.**

QUESTION AND ANSWER

Advise the organisation known as Feminists for Freedom (FFF) on whether its charter's aims entitle it to charitable status.

(i) The FFF seeks to promote a greater understanding of feminist literature, to which end it seeks to publish works by female authors, including books dealing with prostitution. The FFF also seeks to establish a feminist library for FFF staff and their families.

(ii) The FFF seeks to provide accommodation for female single parents on 60-year non-assignable leases at below market price for those who would otherwise be homeless and therefore in need. The FFF does not seek to make a profit from the provision of accommodation and any surplus funds will be used to provide child care facilities for the single mothers.

(iii) The FFF seeks, through lobbying and peaceful demonstration, to change the law relating to gender discrimination and equal pay in this country and abroad and thereby alleviate the lot of all women and improve their life in general.

(iv) The FFF seeks to assist the campaign to allow the ordination of women in the Roman Catholic Church in the belief that this will increase the size of congregations.

(v) The FFF seeks to advance the study by girls and women at schools and institutions of further and higher education in engineering, law, computer sciences, physics and other studies usually associated with men.

Advice and the Answer

In order for the FFF to achieve charitable status, it must show that its objects are exclusively charitable and have a sufficient element of public benefit. It must promote a purpose listed in s.2(2)(a)-(m) of the **Charities Act 2006** or be analogous to such a purpose or have previously been regarded as charitable.

Clause (i): this clause could constitute a trust for the advancement of education: s.2(2)(b). Education is not confined to the classroom (*Re Hopkins*). It is likely that books published by feminists will have a serious social purpose. The library, although educational, would not be charitable as it is restricted to FFF staff and their families. It would therefore not be of general public benefit (*Oppenheim v Tobacco Securities Trust Co Ltd*). As the library is not an ancillary purpose, the whole clause would fail.

Clause (ii): there can be no effective charitable trust under the heading of poverty (s.2(2)(a)) if the gift could benefit the rich as well as the poor (*Re Gwyon*). Single female parents are not necessarily poor, but the facts of the question do state that "they would otherwise be homeless and therefore in need". In *Joseph Rowntree Memorial Trust Housing Association Ltd v Att Gen*, it was held that the fact that the accommodation was provided by way of bargain on a contractual basis, rather than by way of bounty, did not prevent the trust from being charitable. Nor did it matter that the length of the leases might outlast the needs of the beneficiaries as they might well do on the facts of the question. The position would be different if FFF intended to profit from the arrangement and not to use such profit for charitable purposes.

Clause (iii): prima facie this would come within s.2(2)(h) of the **2006 Act** under the head of "the advancement of human rights, conflict resolution or reconciliation or the promotion of religious or racial harmony or equality and diversity". However changing the law is a political purpose and political purposes are not charitable (*McGovern v Att Gen*). This rule applies where the aim is to change the law or government policy at home or abroad.

Clause (iv): it could be argued that this creates a trust for the advancement of religion: s.2(2)(c). Larger congregations mean more people going out into the world to "mix with their fellow citizens" (*Neville Estates Ltd v Madden*). On the other hand, there would need to be a change in canon law to allow women priests and this aim might therefore fail, being tainted with a political purpose.

Clause (v): this would succeed as a trust for education being for the benefit of a sufficiently large section of the community: s.2(2)(b). It does not matter that the trust is for women only.

If any one of the clauses is non-charitable then FFF would not acquire charitable status (*Oxford Group v IRC (1949)*). It would be otherwise if a fully charitable purpose incidentally conferred a benefit on objects that are not charitable (*Re Coxen*). FFF should redraft cl.(ii) so that the library is available to the public at large and delete cll (iii) and (iv). The taxation advantages would make this exercise worthwhile.

The Cy-près Doctrine

12

INTRODUCTION

The term cy-près loosely translated means as near as possible. The cy-près doctrine determines what happens when trust property devoted to charitable purposes cannot be applied in the manner intended by the donor. It is to be remembered that a trust can fail for a variety of reasons, e.g. it might be illegal, impossible or impracticable to carry out the settlor's wishes. In private trusts, this will give rise to a resulting trust in favour of the settlor or his estate. This is, however, not always so with charitable trusts because the courts have both an inherent jurisdiction and an extended statutory jurisdiction (ss.13 and 14 of the Charities Act 1993 as amended) to invoke the cy-près doctrine. The doctrine allows them to apply the funds to similar charitable bodies or charitable purposes which, of course, differ to the original charitable purposes.

INHERENT JURISDICTION

Meaning
The court's inherent jurisdiction is limited and can be claimed only where the performance of the trust is impossible or impractical. Unlike the statutory jurisdiction, it does not operate when the trust is cumbersome, inconvenient or uneconomical. Impossibility or impracticability may be apparent from the outset, or it may become clear at some later date that the charitable purpose cannot be carried into effect.

KEY CASES

ATT GEN V CITY OF LONDON (1790) AND RE LYSAGHT (1966)
In *Att Gen v City of London* (1790), the trust included the advancement and propagation of the Christian religion among the infidels of Virginia. It was held that the purpose had become impossible as there were no infidels left in Virginia. Cy-près was allowed.

A creative use of cy-près occurred in *Re Lysaght* (1966). The testatrix provided funds to found medical scholarships to be run by the Royal College of Surgeons. One of the terms was that the awards were not to

Figure 13: Cy-Près

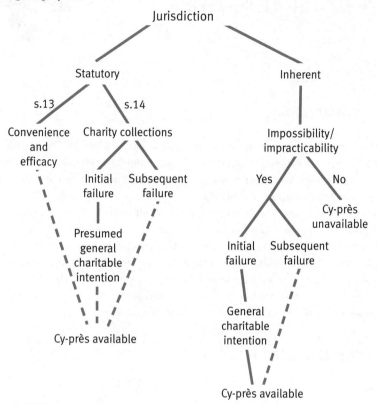

be made to Jews or Roman Catholics. The Royal College refused to accept the gift on these terms so it became impractical to carry out the trust. The court, therefore, deleted the religious discrimination clause.

Initial Failure and Finding a General Charitable Intention

Many gifts to specific charities fail because the charity has ceased to exist or the purpose has become impossible before the date of the gift. This is called initial impossibility. In these cases, the trust property can be applied cy-près under a scheme drawn up by the courts or the Charity Commission provided that the settlor had a general charitable intention. The need for a general charitable intention means that, if the gift is solely for a particular purpose, it will fail and leave no room for cy-près.

RE RYMER (1895), RE SPENCE (1979), BISCOE V JACKSON (1887) AND
RE HARWOOD (1936)

- In *Re Rymer* (1895), there was a specific intention to benefit a seminary for priests that no longer existed. There could be no cy-près because it was viewed as a gift to a particular body for a particular purpose.
- In *Re Spence* (1979), there was initial failure of a gift to a named old people's home that had ceased to exist. As the gift could not be construed as being to the old in the area, there was no general charitable intention.
- In *Biscoe v Jackson* (1887), money was set aside to finance a soup kitchen and a cottage hospital in Shoreditch. It was not possible to build the hospital, but the money was applied cy-près because the specified purposes were only two methods of helping the poor of Shoreditch. The charitable intention was general and not specific or limited.
- In *Re Harwood* (1936), one gift was made in favour of the Belfast Peace Society and another in favour of the Wisbech Peace Society. The Belfast Peace Society had never existed. The court allowed the application of the gift cy-près because only a general charitable intention could be attributed to a donor who incorrectly identified the beneficiary of the gift. The other gift could not be applied cy-près. It is much more difficult to identify a general charitable intention when the charity specified is correctly identified, but has since ceased to exist.

Continuation in another form

A named charity may have ceased to function, but may still be continuing in another form. It may, for example, have been amalgamated or reconstituted under different trusts. In *Re Faraker* (1912), a gift to Mrs Bailey's Charity, Rotherhithe passed into the hands of a new body that was created by an amalgamation of that charity and several others. The legacy was applied cy-près for the consolidated charities. Similarly, in *Re Finger's Will Trusts* (1972) one gift was to the National Radium Commission (an unincorporated association) and another to the National Council for Maternity and Child Welfare (an incorporated body). When the testatrix died both bodies had ceased to exist (i.e. there was initial impossibility). The purposes of the National Radium Commission continued to exist and the gift was held to be a gift to those purposes. It did not matter that the donee no longer existed. The gift to the incorporated body prima facie should have failed. It was a gift to that particular body and not a trust for its purposes.

The court, however, found on the particular facts of the case that the testatrix had a paramount charitable intention and so the gift was applied cy-près.

List of objects

When a failed charitable gift is one of a number of other charitable gifts in the same document (e.g. the same will), the traditional rule is that this association does not make it easier to discern a general charitable intention: *Re Jenkins (1966)*. There a non-charitable object was specified. As Buckley J. admitted, "if you meet seven men with black hair and one with red hair you are not entitled to say that there are eight men with black hair". Conversely, in *Re Satthertewaite's Will Trust* (1966) eight animal charities were selected at random from the phone book. One had never existed, but the court was able to infer a general charitable intention and apply the money cy-près.

Subsequent Failure

Meaning

A charity might cease to exist after the property has become vested in the charity. This is known as subsequent failure. The cy-près doctrine will apply here irrespective of whether or not there is a general charitable intention. Accordingly, there is no chance of a resulting trust to the donor.

KEY CASES

RE SLEVIN (1891) AND RE KING (1923)

- In *Re Slevin* (1891), money was dedicated to an orphanage. Although the orphanage was in existence at the testator's death, it ceased to operate before the money came into its hands. Nevertheless, the money had become legally vested in it on the testator's death. This was considered a straightforward case of subsequent failure and the money was applied cy-près.

- In *Re King* (1923), a gift was made to provide a stained glass window in a church. On completion of the work, there remained a residue of over £1,000. It was held that this surplus could be applied cy-près even though there was no general charitable intention shown by the donor.

Timing

The time for deciding whether there is an initial or subsequent failure is at the time of the gift. In the case of a will, the relevant date is that of the testator's death. If the gift is possible at that time, but becomes impossible before it is available for the charity, it still counts as a case of subsequent impossibility. In *Re Wright* (1954), the testatrix died in 1933 leaving her residuary estate to a tenant for life, the remainder to be used to found a house for convalescent and impecunious gentlewomen. By the time the life tenant died in 1942, it was impracticable to found the home. The court found that dedication to charity occurred in 1933 and so the gift could be applied cy-près without the need of finding any paramount charitable intent.

STATUTORY JURISDICTION

Section 13 of the Charities Act 1993
Cy-près is no longer confined only to cases where it is "impossible" or "impracticable" to implement the terms of the trust. Section 13 extends the circumstances in which cy-près is available and allows cy-près on the basis of convenience and efficacy. Section 13 prescribes certain situations where cy-près is appropriate. The **Charities Act 2006** has amended s.13 to take into account not only the spirit of the gift, but also social and economic circumstances prevailing at the time of the proposed alteration of the original purposes.

Where the original purposes have been fulfilled
In *Re Lepton's Charity* (1972), a will dated 1715 directed that £3 per annum was to be paid to the local minister and any surplus income to the poor. By 1970, the trust income had risen from £5 to £800. The court increased the minister's stipend to £100 per annum. Modern conditions entailed that £3 was not in keeping with the spirit of the gift.

Where the original purposes provide a use for part only of the donated money
In *Re North Devon and West Somerset Relief Fund* (1953), surplus funds raised for those who suffered in the floods in 1952 were applicable cy-près. The contributors had parted with their money out and out and did not intend that the surplus, if any, would be returned to them should the immediate object of charity come to an end. The original purposes provided a use for part only of the property.

Where the property will be more effectively used in conjunction with other property
This would cover the situation as in *Re Faraker* (1912) where Mrs Bayley's Charity (established to provide for poor widows of Rotherhithe) was amalgamated with 13 other charities each of which benefited the poor.

Where the original purposes were laid down by reference to an area or by reference to a class of persons which has for any reason since ceased to exist or to be suitable

In *Peggs v Lamb* (1994), a cy-près scheme was authorised in circumstances where a charitable purpose, which was originally for the benefit of the freemen of a borough, was enlarged to cover the inhabitants of the borough as a whole. This was because those who would qualify as freemen had declined in numbers to 15 and the income to be distributed had risen to £559,000 per annum.

Where the original purposes, in whole or in part, have been adequately provided for by other means; ceased to be charitable; or ceased to provide a suitable and effective method of using the property donated

The court enabled a gift to be divided between two conflicting groups of a Hindu sect in *Varsani v Jesani* (1998). The charity had divided into two factions and it became impossible to achieve the original purposes that had been envisaged. The property (a temple) was not, therefore, being used in accordance with the spirit of the gift.

Section 14: Charity Collections
Context
Problems can arise in the context of funds raised by public appeal for a charitable purpose where it is impossible or impracticable to apply the property to that purpose or where a purpose has been achieved leaving a surplus. Section 14 of the **Charities Act 1993** is designed to cover this situation and applies when the money has been donated through collecting boxes, lotteries, competitions and so forth.

Presumption
Section 14 provides that property donated for specific charitable purposes which fail can be applicable cy-près as though the donation was for general charitable purposes. As such, the section caters for the situation where it is difficult or impossible to locate the donors. There is a presumption, in relation to cash collections and fund-raising events, that the donors are unidentifiable. It is important to appreciate that the section applies to cases of initial failure. There can never be the return of the property in cases of subsequent failure.

Section 14A: Solicited Gifts
This provision is inserted by the **Charities Act 2006** and applies to property given for specific charitable purposes in response to a solicitation (e.g. an advertisement or letter). If the solicitation is accompanied by a statement

to the effect that, if the purposes fail, the property will be applied cy-près, then this will prevail. The exception to this is when the donor makes a written declaration that he may want the money returned if the purpose fails.

You should now know and understand:

- the meaning and role of cy-près;

- the inherent jurisdiction of the court;

- the distinction between initial and subsequent failure;

- the meaning of a general charitable intention;

- the statutory jurisdiction.

QUESTION AND ANSWER

The Question

In the context of the cy-près doctrine what is the concept of a general charitable intention and why may it matter whether the failure of trust is classified as either "initial" or "subsequent"?

Advice and the Answer

This is a straightforward question which requires a straightforward answer. The answer should open with an explanation of the cy-près doctrine and a general consideration of the statutory and inherent jurisdictions of the court. It should be noted that the statutory jurisdiction was intended to widen the scope of cy-près.

It then is necessary to explain the meaning of the phrase a general charitable intention and illustrate how it may be established with case law examples (e.g. *Rymer* (1895); *Spence* (1979) and *Harwood* (1936)). The issue of when the concept assumes relevance must then be addressed. The important point to make is that a general charitable intention need only be considered in cases of initial failure.

As a general charitable intention enjoys no relevance as regards subsequent failure, it is necessary to make the distinction from initial failure. Cases such as *King* (1923); *Slevin* (1891) and *Wright* (1954) offer good illustrations of a subsequent failure. In relation to s.14 of the **Charities Act 1993** (as amended) as it applies to general charity collections, the possibility of initial failure is dealt with. In order to prevent the money having to be returned to the donors, s.14 presumes a general charitable intention on the basis that the identity of the donors cannot be ascertained.

Appointment, Retirement and Removal of Trustees

13

INTRODUCTION

The trustee is the central figure in the administration of the trust. The trustee labours under onerous obligations in order to protect the trust property, give effect to the settlor's instructions and promote the interests of the beneficiary. The choice and appointment of the trustee is, therefore, a key matter in the creation and administration of the trust. In time, it may be that a serving trustee may wish to retire (e.g. due to old age or illness) or is removed (e.g. due to incompetence or dishonesty) and a replacement trustee is required. This Chapter considers how trustees are appointed and how they may be removed whether voluntarily and involuntarily.

CAPACITY AND NUMBER

Generally any person who has the capacity to hold property can be a trustee. A minor cannot be appointed a trustee nor can he hold a legal estate in land: the **Law of Property Act 1925**, s.20. Infancy is, moreover, one of the grounds for removing a trustee and appointing another under s.36(1) of the **Trustee Act 1925**. A minor may, however, be a trustee of personal property held on an implied trust. In *Re Vinogradoff* (1935), a grandmother put War Loan stock into the names of herself and her granddaughter. The granddaughter was only four years old. It was held that, as there was no presumption of advancement in the child's favour, she became a trustee holding the property on a resulting trust for her grandmother.

Corporations

A corporation can be a trustee. Some corporations are known as trust corporations. These include the Public Trustee, the Treasury Solicitor, the Official Solicitor, certain charitable or public corporations and those corporations entitled to act as custodian trustees under the Public Trustee Act 1906.

Numbers

In a trust or settlement of land, the maximum permitted number of trustees is four. The minimum number is one trustee. In order to ensure that trust interests are overreached (i.e. taken free of) by a purchaser, however, the purchase money must be paid to at least two trustees or a trust corporation. Hence, if there is a sole trustee of land, the prospective purchaser should require an additional trustee to be appointed. The trustees of land must always hold the legal title as joint tenants. This means that, if one dies, the surviving trustees continue until only one remains alive. As regards a trust of personal property, there is no limit to the number of trustees who can be appointed.

APPOINTMENT OF TRUSTEES

There is a general equitable principle that a trust will not fail want for a trustee. This means that a trust will not fail if, for example, the appointed trustees refuse to act or have ceased to exist. If necessary, the Public Trustee will act in the capacity of trustee. An exception to this rule arises when the trust is made conditional upon certain people acting as trustees: *Hill v Royal College of Surgeons* (1966).

Original Trustees

As regards the initial trustees, they are generally appointed in a will or settlement. The settlor chooses who he wishes to be trustee. When one of the initial trustees dies, the property vests in the survivor(s). On the death of the last survivor, the property vests in his personal representative, who holds subject to the trust: s.18 of the **Trustee Act 1925**.

New Trustees

As soon as the trust is created, the settlor has no automatic right to appoint future trustees. The authority to appoint replacement trustees can arise either from an express power, a statutory power or on the order of the court.

* The trust instrument may reserve for the settlor or some other person the express power to appoint new trustees. This is a common practice and will dictate the terms and mode of the appointment.
* Under the statutory power afforded by s.36 of the **Trustee Act 1925** replacement and/or additional trustees may be appointed.
* By virtue of the more limited statutory power, beneficiaries may appoint under ss.19 and 20 of the **Trusts of Land and Appointment of Trustees Act 1996** (TLATA).
* As a last resort, the court appointment of new trustees is permitted under s.41 of the **Trustee Act 1925**.

Figure 14: Appointment, Retirement and Removal of Trustees

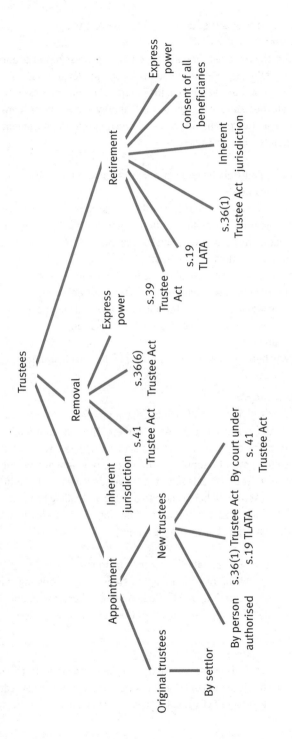

Appointment under s.36 of the **Trustee Act 1925**

Replacement Trustees

Although the trust instrument may confer an express power of appointment of trustees, reliance is placed (usually by the settlor or trustees) on the wide statutory power as set out in s.36. The trust instrument, however, will usually nominate those who may exercise the statutory power. Unless there is a contrary provision in the trust instrument, s.36 provides that a replacement trustee may be appointed when a trustee:

- has died (this includes a person appointed in a will who dies before the testator);
- has remained outside the UK for a continuous period exceeding 12 months. This ground is often expressly excluded where for tax reasons all the trust property is outside the UK;
- seeks to retire from the trust;
- refuses to act or disclaims the role before accepting office;
- is unfit to act (e.g. where he has become bankrupt);
- is incapable of acting. This includes physical and mental illness, old age and, in the case of a corporation, dissolution;
- is an infant; or
- has been removed under a power in the trust instrument.

Statutory purpose

The aim of s.36 is not only to enable the appointment of a new trustee without a court order, but also to ensure that there will be someone who has the ability to exercise the power if necessary. It sets out a hierarchy of persons who may exercise the power to appoint. If there is no one able and willing to exercise the power in the first category, the power devolves to those in the second category and so on. If there is no person able and willing to act, the s.36 power necessarily becomes redundant. The following characters in the following pecking order have the ability to engage s.36:

- the person nominated in the trust instrument;
- the "surviving or continuing" trustees (i.e. the existing trustees). This caters for a retiring trustee to nominate his successor; and
- the personal representatives of the last surviving trustee.

Additional trustees

Traditionally, and unless the trust instrument provided to the contrary, an additional trustee could only be appointed when there was a vacancy. Section 36(6) of the **Trustee Act 1925**, however, caters generally for the appointment in writing of additional trustees (i.e. without any replacement). The appointment may be made by the person nominated by the trust instrument to appoint new trustees or, if there is no such person able and willing to act, the trustee(s) for the time being. Section 36(6), however, only permits an additional appointment when there are no more than three existing trustees (i.e. the general rule is that the number of trustees cannot be increased beyond four). While as regards trusts of personalty the trust instrument itself may increase this number, the maximum ceiling for trusts of land must always remain at four trustees.

The Trusts of Land and Appointment of Trustees Act 1996

Where all the beneficiaries are sui juris (i.e. of full age and capacity) they may act in unison and direct the current trustees to appoint in writing any person(s) of the beneficiaries' collective choosing as trustee(s): s.19(1). The appointment is, thereby, effected by the existing trustees. If there are none remaining, the direction must be given to the personal representative of the last surviving trustee. This power applies retrospectively to trusts of all types of property. The power can be excluded in the trust instrument, for example, when a power to appoint trustees is vested in someone nominated for the purpose in the trust instrument. Hence, it is designed to apply only when the trust instrument makes no provision for the appointment of new trustees. Unlike the power granted under s.36 of the **Trustee Act**, the appointment of new trustees under s.19 is not tied to such occurrences as death, unfitness, incapacity and the like. The power can, moreover, be exercised as often as the beneficiaries may deem appropriate.

Mental disorder

Section 20 of the **1996 Act** deals with the situation where a trustee is rendered incapable of carrying out his office by reason of a mental disorder and there is no person willing or able to appoint a replacement under an express power of appointment or under s.36. In this situation, s.20 enables the beneficiaries of full age and capacity in unison to direct the appointment of a replacement trustee. Again this provision can be excluded in the trust instrument.

Appointment by the Court

The court has a statutory jurisdiction to appoint replacement or additional trustees under s.41 of the **Trustee Act 1925**. This offers the court a broad, discretionary power to appoint new trustees in circumstances where it is "inexpedient, difficult or impracticable so to do without the assistance of the court". It does not have to be "necessary" for the court to act. An order can be made on the application of either a trustee or beneficiary. The court will not usually make an appointment when there is an express power in the trust instrument or where one of the other statutory powers can be employed. Accordingly, the s.41 power tends to be exercised only in situations where there is doubt as to whether a trustee is "unfit" or "incapable" to act. It has, however, been employed in circumstances where the trustee has emigrated, when there is no one who has the power to make an appointment and where the intention is to increase the number of trustees beyond four.

Vesting of Trust Property

On their appointment, the trust property has to become vested in the new trustees. Section 40 of the **Trustee Act 1925** provides that, where the trustee is appointed by deed, a vesting declaration in the deed will operate to vest the property in the new trustees. Such a declaration may be implied, subject to any provision in the deed to the contrary. There is, therefore, no need for an express conveyance or assignment.

Section 40 does not apply to:
* land held by trustees on a mortgage as security for a loan of trust money. This means that, where trust money is invested in the mortgage of land, on the appointment of new trustees automatic vesting does not occur. Instead, there must be a separate, formal transfer of the mortgage term to the new trustee;
* land held under a lease or sub-lease that contains a covenant against assignment without consent, unless the consent has been obtained before the execution of the deed. This exemption prevents the appointment of a trustee causing an inadvertent breach of covenant against assignment and giving rise to a forfeiture of the lease;
* stocks and shares. This exception recognises that the legal title to shares can only be effected by registration with the relevant company, and
* registered land. Section 27 of the Land Registration Act 2002 requires that the deed of appointment/retirement must be registered so that the change of registered proprietor can be duly recorded.

TERMINATING TRUSTEESHIP

Disclaimer
A person is not bound to accept the onerous duties of a trustee just because he is named in a trust instrument or because he has previously agreed to be a trustee. He must, however, disclaim before he has done any act indicating acceptance. He cannot disclaim part only of the trust: *Re Lord Fullertons Contract* (1896). When disclaiming a trust it is advisable, albeit not essential, to do so by deed. If the trustee disclaiming is the sole trustee, the trust property will result to the settlor or his personal representatives upon trust. If there are other trustees the property will remain with them.

Retirement
A trustee may retire only in one of six ways:

- by virtue of a special power in the trust instrument. If express provision is made for retirement, the trustee can, of course, exercise that power;
- under s.36(1) of the **Trustee Act 1925** when a replacement trustee is being appointed;
- under s.39 of the **1925 Act**. This statutory escape is not, however, dependent upon the appointment of a replacement trustee. It allows a trustee to retire if there will remain at least two other trustees or a trust corporation in office. It is also necessary that the remaining trustees consent to the retirement and that the consent of any person who has an express power to appoint trustees has been obtained;
- with the consent of all the beneficiaries who must all be of full age and ability. If there is an infant beneficiary, therefore, no effective discharge can arise in this way;
- by virtue of an order of the court under s.41 of the **Trustee Act 1925** when the trustee is being replaced by a new appointment, and
- the court also enjoys an inherent jurisdiction to discharge a trustee without nominating any replacement. This is useful when the consent of the other trustees cannot be obtained for the purposes of s.39. The court will usually accede to the trustee's wish to retire.

DIRECTION BY BENEFICIARIES TO RETIRE

Sections 19–21 of the Trusts of Land and Appointment of Trustees Act 1996 provide that beneficiaries (who are unanimous, of full age and capacity and between them entitled to the whole beneficial interest) may direct the retirement of a trustee. The conditions for the compulsory pensioning off of a trustee are:

- there must be no person nominated by the trust instrument who has the power to appoint new trustees;
- a written direction must be given to the trustee;
- reasonable arrangements must be made for the protection of any rights of the trustee in connection with the trust;
- on the trustee's retirement there must remain a trust corporation or at least two trustees;
- a new trustee must be appointed on his retirement or, if no such appointment is to be made, the continuing trustees must consent by deed to his retirement;

- the retiring trustee must execute a deed of discharge (he has the ability to defer the deed until reasonable arrangements for his protection have been made); and
- the retiring and continuing trustees and any new trustee must do anything necessary to vest the trust property in the continuing and new trustees.

Removal under the Court's Inherent Jurisdiction

The High Court enjoys an inherent jurisdiction to control the administration of a trust and the actions of the trustee. The overarching duty is to see that trusts are properly executed. To this end, the court may remove a trustee on the application of any beneficiary. Indeed, it can remove a trustee of its own volition during proceedings. The inherent jurisdiction is particularly useful when there is a dispute as to the facts and/or no replacement is to be made. For example, in *Letterstedt v Broers* (1884) a beneficiary made a number of allegations of misconduct against the trustees and asked for their removal. Although the allegations were unfounded, he succeeded in his application. It was held that the duty of the court was to ensure the proper execution of the trust. Even if the facts are disputed, or the trustees can disprove the allegations, they may still be removed if there is disharmony as to the manner in which the trust is to be administered.

Beneficiary's welfare

The welfare of the beneficiary is the paramount concern and the court must, therefore, evaluate whether the trustee's continuance in office would be prejudicial to the interests of the beneficiaries. Accordingly, the court can consider the expense to the trust of a change of trustees and, even where there has been a minor breach of trust, decide against removal: *Re Wrightson* (1908). This case shows that reasonable cause must be established to justify the removal. A trustee who sets up a rival business might not be in breach of trust, but the conflict of interest would be a ground for his removal: *Moore v M'Glynn* (1896).

Revision Checklist

You should now know and understand:

- **how original trustees are appointed;**
- **how replacement and additional trustees are appointed;**
- **how trust property vests in the trustee;**
- **how trustees may retire or be removed.**

QUESTION AND ANSWER

Consider the purpose and operation of s.36 of the **Trustee Act 1925** and explain how it impacts upon the appointment and replacement of trustees.

By way of an introduction, the essay should open with a statement of context. It should note that trustees may be appointed both on the creation of a trust and during its continuance, whether as replacement for an existing trustee or in addition to the existing trustees. It should also make clear that, as soon as the trust is created, the settlor has no automatic right to appoint future trustees. The authority to appoint new replacement trustees can arise either from an express power, a statutory power or on the order of the court. Section 36 affords the major statutory power to appoint replacement and/or additional trustees. This provision enables the appointment of a new trustee without a court order and ensures that there will be someone who has the ability to exercise the power if necessary. It focuses upon the appointment of replacement and additional trustees.

As regards replacement trustees, s.36(1) makes clear that the appointment has to be "in place of" a retiring trustee. This entails that the appointment of one new trustee will never be sufficient to discharge two retiring trustees. One trustee can, therefore, only replace another trustee. Retirement can occur under s.36(1) when a replacement trustee is being appointed. Similarly, the removal of a trustee can occur under s.36(1) only on the appointment of a replacement trustee. Section 36(1) can, however, operate only limited circumstances and these are where a trustee (whether an original trustee or not):

- has died;
- has, for whatever reason, remained outside the UK for a continuous period of more than 12 months;
- has expressed the wish to be discharged from the trust;
- has refused or has become unfit to act as trustee or has become incapable of acting as trustee; or,
- is an infant.

As to who can exercise the power to appoint, s.36 lists the following characters in the order of priority:

- the person nominated in the trust instrument as having the right to appoint new trustees;
- the existing trustees;
- the personal representatives of the last surviving trustee.

Traditionally, and unless the trust instrument provided to the contrary, an additional trustee could only be appointed when there was a vacancy. Section 36(6), however, caters generally for the appointment in writing of additional trustees (i.e. without any replacement). The appointment may be made by the person nominated by the trust instrument to appoint new trustees or, if there is no such person able and willing to act, the trustee(s) for the time being. Section 36(6), however, only permits an additional appointment when there are no more than three existing trustees (i.e. the general rule is that the number of trustees cannot be increased beyond four). While as regards trusts of personalty the trust instrument may increase the number, the maximum ceiling for trusts of land must always remain at four trustees.

Trustee's Duties

14

....

INTRODUCTION

The duties of a trustee are extremely onerous. They have to be carried out with the utmost diligence. If not, the trustee may be personally liable for breach of trust. Some duties arise automatically from the relationship between trustee and beneficiary while others are imposed and regulated by statute. Central to the trustee's functions is the fiduciary duty that is imposed by equity. This places an obligation of loyalty and faithfulness upon the shoulders of a trustee. The fiduciary duty entails that, put simply, the trustee must act in utmost good faith.

....

DUTIES ON APPOINTMENT

Upon accepting the office, the trustee is expected to ascertain the terms of the trust and to confirm that he has been validly appointed and that the trust property has been vested in him. In addition, the trustee labours under several other administrative duties.

Safeguarding Trust Property
If the trust was in existence before his appointment, a new trustee must ensure the trust property has been properly invested. If a trust investment has fallen in value and threatens to jeopardise the trust fund, the trustee should consider whether to reinvest elsewhere. Otherwise, he will be liable for the failure to review. In *Re Medland* (1889), trust money was lent on mortgage, but the security for the loan had depreciated in value and now risked the interests of the trust. It was held that the trustee should have deliberated whether or not to call in the mortgage. Except where expressly allowed in the trust instrument, the trustee should never lend trust money or allow it to remain outstanding on an unsecured basis. If the trust property includes chattels, the trustee should also obtain an accurate inventory. The trustee is expected to ensure that all securities and chattels are in safe custody. As regards land, the trustee should ensure that it is secure and free from the adverse claims of a trespasser.

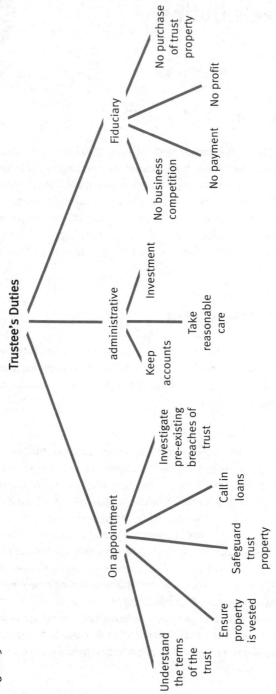

Trustee's Duties

On appointment
- Understand the terms of the trust
- Ensure property is vested
- Safeguard trust property
- Call in loans
- Investigate pre-existing breaches of trust

administrative
- Keep accounts
- Take reasonable care
- Investment

Fiduciary
- No business competition
- No payment
- No profit
- No purchase of trust property

Figure 15

Calling in Loans

The trustee should ensure that, where part of the trust property is a loan due for repayment, this loan should be called in. This action is required because of the general notion that the trustee must take all reasonable steps to safeguard trust assets. The danger for the trustee is that, if he allows the debt to become statute-barred under the Limitation Act 1980, he will assume personal liability for the ensuing loss to the trust. If necessary, therefore, the trustee must institute legal action to enforce repayment.

Legal action

The trustee who decides not to bring an enforcement action should ask the court for directions under s.57 of the **Trustee Act 1925** that support the intended inaction. If not, the trustee might show that he held a well-founded belief that any enforcement action would be pointless. It is, however, no defence for the trustee to argue that he thought it somehow indelicate or inappropriate to ask for the loan to be repaid and to initiate recovery proceedings: *Re Brogden* (1888).

Joint Control

The trust property ought to be placed in the joint control of all the trustees. It must be kept distinct from the trustee's personal property or the property of any other trust. Accordingly, a new trustee should ensure that investments are in the names of all the trustees. If not, and where trust property is misapplied by a trustee, the co-trustees are potentially liable for any loss that arises. In *Lewis v Nobbs* (1878), the trust property included bearer bonds which were in the sole control of one trustee. When this trustee went off with the bonds in his custody, the other trustee was held liable because by his negligence he had facilitated the misappropriation.

Custodians

In order to protect themselves, trustees are now given the right by the **Trustee Act 2000** to appoint custodians of trust property and documents. Indeed, in relation to so-called bearer securities (i.e. securities which are not registered in the name of anyone), the trustees must appoint a custodian unless exempted by the trust instrument or by statutory provision.

....

GENERAL FIDUCIARY DUTIES

> **DEFINITION CHECKPOINT**
>
> The trustee/beneficiary relationship is not the only type of fiduciary relationship. The classic examples of fiduciary relationships are as between principal and agent, director and company and partner and

co-partner. A fiduciary relationship emerges where one party undertakes to act in relation to the property or affairs of another in circumstances that give rise to a relationship of **trust and confidence.** The fiduciary owes core duties of **loyalty and fidelity.** Breach of fiduciary duty, therefore, connotes disloyalty and infidelity. Mere incompetence is not enough: *Bristol & West Building Society v Mothew* (1998).

Duty not to make a Profit

The trustee may not make an unauthorised profit from his position as trustee. He must not put himself in a position where his duty to the trust and his own personal interest may conflict. In *Keech v Sandford* (1726), a trustee of a lease applied for its renewal for the benefit of an infant beneficiary. It was refused, but the landlord agreed to renew the lease in the trustee's own favour. There was no question of fraud, but it was concluded that the trustee held the lease on trust for the infant. The reason was that there would be less incentive on the trustee to press for a renewal for the trust if he knew that he would benefit by a refusal. The rule in *Keech v Sandford*, however, applies only when a trustee or some other fiduciary obtains the benefit.

Bribes

Understandably, where the trustee has acted in bad faith, and by doing so made a profit, he will have to account for that profit. In *Reading v Att Gen* (1951), an army sergeant earned £19,000 by transporting smuggled goods in an army vehicle and while in army uniform. The profit was confiscated and, on his release from prison, he took action for its return. His action failed because he was a fiduciary and was liable to account for the profits to the Crown. Similarly, in *Att Gen for Hong Kong v Reid* (1994) a fiduciary accepted bribes during the course of his employment by the Crown. It was held that the Crown was able to claim the property acquired by the bribes (three houses) even though the houses were now of a higher value than the bribes received.

Purchase of Trust Property

Traditionally, the prevention of a trustee from purchasing trust property was classified as merely one aspect of the trustee's duty not to profit from his position. The modern approach, however, is to view this type of purchase as being the subject of two distinct rules, namely, the self-dealing rule and the insider dealing rule (sometimes known also as the fair dealing rule).

Self-dealing rule

Subject to any contrary provision in the trust instrument, the purchase of trust property by a trustee is voidable by any beneficiary. The notion is that the trustee should not profit from his office and it reflects the possibility that the trustee might not give the best price obtainable. This self-dealing rule applies to all types of property and a transaction can be set aside as against the trustee as well as against any purchaser from the trustee who has notice of the breach of trust. A transaction is tainted by the self-dealing rule even in the absence of unfairness or sharp practice and regardless of whether or not the trustee makes a profit. A beneficiary's ability to set aside the transaction applies even if the property was bought at a public auction: *Ex p. Lacey* (1802).

Insider dealing (fair dealing) rule
A different approach is adopted when the trustee or other fiduciary intends to purchase the equitable interest of a beneficiary, e.g. the trustee wishes to buy out the beneficiary's interest in land. Whereas the self-dealing rule is based upon the relationship between the parties, the fiduciary rule against insider dealing is framed around the conduct of the trustee. In order for the sale to be effective, the transaction must be fair and honest. This means that the consideration provided must be adequate, there must be no undue influence exerted by the trustee and the beneficiary must be given full and accurate information about the extent of the beneficial interest to be bought: *Tito v Waddell (No. 2)* (1977).

> It is a relevant factor that it is the beneficiary who initiated the sale. In *Coles v Trecothick* (1804), the sale was upheld in circumstances where the beneficiary took control of the sale by auction. The beneficiary had chosen both the venue and the auctioneer and, moreover, was content with the price obtained on the sale. In contrast, in *Dougan v Macpherson* (1902) two brothers were beneficiaries under a trust. One brother was also a trustee. The trustee purchased his brother's beneficial interest without disclosing to him a valuation report of the trust estate. The beneficial share was worth much more than the trustee paid for it. The transaction here was set aside.

Remunerative Employment
A trustee must not use his position in order to obtain paid employment. Similar principles apply to such characters as bankers, company directors and business partners. They are accountable for any profits they make because of their position. In *Williams v Barton* (1927), a stockbroker trustee had to hand over to the trust the commission he earned on valuation by his firm of the trust assets. Often a trustee will obtain remuneration as a director of a company. If the directorship was acquired because of his position as a trustee, he will be accountable to the

trust: *Re Macadam* (1946). This is not so, however, if the trustees were directors before they became trustees (*Re Dover Coalfield Extension Ltd* (1908)) or if the trustees were appointed directors without any reliance on the trust votes (*Re Gee* (1948)). The will or settlement may, moreover, authorise the trustee to keep any remuneration: *Re Llewellin's Will Trusts* (1949).

Other Abuses of Position

- In *Industrial Development Consultants Ltd v Cooley* (1971), a managing director of a company had been negotiating a contract with the Eastern Gas Board. The Gas Board did not wish to enter into any dealings with the company, but it was prepared to enter a contract with the managing director privately. Consequently, he terminated his association with the company on the false basis of illness and signed the contract with the Gas Board. Although a contract between the company and the Gas Board would never have come to fruition, its former managing director had to account to the company for the benefit of the contract he had personally entered.

- In *Regal (Hastings) Ltd v Gulliver* (1942), the directors of Regal wished to buy two further motion picture theatres for the company. As Regal could fund only £2,000 of the required £5,000, the directors decided to club together and to raise the shortfall themselves. The purchase went ahead, the directors sold their shares in Regal and made a substantial profit. Although the directors argued that they had acted in good faith and had secured a benefit for Regal, it was held by the House of Lords that the directors were liable to account to the Company for the profits made.

- In *Boardman v Phipps* (1967), Mr Boardman (the trust solicitor) became concerned about a trust investment in a failing private company. He concluded that the only way to protect the trust investment was for the trust to obtain a majority shareholding in the company and to appoint a new management. As the trustees were unwilling to do this, he and one of the beneficiaries went off and bought the outstanding shares themselves. Mr Boardman had claimed to represent the trust and had obtained information that was not available to the public at large. The trust benefited by £47,000 and Mr Boardman and the beneficiary made a profit in the region of £75,000. The profit had been made by the use of information that had been acquired by the pair while acting on behalf of the trust and in a fiduciary capacity. The pair had to account to the trust for the profit made.

Payment for Acting as Trustee

One of the consequences of the rule that a trustee must not make a profit from his trust is that, unless authorised in the trust deed or approved by all the beneficiaries sui juris, a trustee cannot charge for his time and trouble: *Barrett v Hartley* (1866). Even a solicitor trustee cannot charge for anything other than his out-of-pocket expenses. There are, however, exceptions to this rule.

Special trustees
The court has a statutory jurisdiction to authorise payment where it appoints a corporation to be a trustee: s.42 of the Trustee Act 1925. A Judicial Trustee may be paid out of trust property: s.1(5) of the **Judicial Trustees Act 1896.** The Public Trustee or a custodian trustee can charge under the **Public Trustee Act 1906**.

Inherent jurisdiction
The court has an inherent jurisdiction to allow a trustee to be paid where there is no charging clause in the trust instrument. Alternatively, it can vary or increase the amount that can be charged when there is a charging clause. The services of the trustee must, however, be regarded as being of exceptional benefit to the trust. In *Re Duke of Norfolk's Settlement* (1981), a trust corporation accepted the administration of the trust for a low annual fee. As trustee, it subsequently became involved in an extensive redevelopment project and was allowed an increase in remuneration because the duties became unexpectedly onerous.

Solicitor's litigation costs
Solicitor-trustees' costs of litigation are the subject of special treatment. According to the rule in *Cradock v Piper* (1850), a solicitor-trustee is entitled to profit costs in litigation where he acts as solicitor for himself and a co-trustee in relation to the trust. This is provided that the costs are no more than they would have been had he acted for the co-trustee alone. A solicitor-trustee cannot employ his firm to do non-litigious work.

Trustee Act 2000
Where there is no entitlement to remuneration given by the trust instrument or by another statutory provision, s.29 of the **Trustee Act 2000** offers additional entitlements. First, a trustee that is a trust corporation is entitled to reasonable remuneration. Secondly, a trustee who acts in a professional capacity is also entitled to reasonable remuneration provided that each of the other trustees agrees in writing. Section 29, therefore, does not apply if there is a sole trustee.

Out of Pocket Expenses
A trustee is entitled to be reimbursed for out of pocket expenses such as insurance premiums, fees paid to brokers and money spent on repairs. Section 31(1) of the **Trustee Act 2000** provides that a trustee has a right to recover "expenses properly incurred by him when acting on the behalf of the trust". A trustee will

also be allowed his litigation costs if the court grants leave to sue or defend. In other cases, the trustee will obtain costs only if the action was properly brought or defended for the benefit of the trust estate: *Holding & Management Ltd v Property Holding & Investment Trusts Plc* (1990).

Business Competition

If the trust contains a business as part of its assets then the trustee should not compete. In *Re Thompson* (1930), the trust property included a yacht broker's business. A trustee wanted to set up a similar business in the same locality. The court issued an injunction restraining the trustee because his plans would have taken trade away from the trust business.

DUTY TO KEEP ACCOUNTS AND PROVIDE INFORMATION

Trustees must keep clear and accurate accounts and produce them to any beneficiary when required. A beneficiary is entitled to all reasonable information about the administration of the trust. When a beneficiary reaches 18 years of age, he should be informed of his interest under the trust. Section 22(4) of the **Trustee Act 1925** gives the trustees an absolute discretion to have the accounts audited by an independent accountant, but no more than once in every three years unless there are special circumstances.

Trust Documents

Beneficiaries are entitled to see all trust documents and title deeds: *O'Rourke v Darbishire* (1920). Not all documents held by trustees, however, are "trust documents". Trustees are not bound to give reasons why they have exercised their discretion in a particular way: *Schmidt v Rosewood Trust Ltd* (2003). Hence, they are not bound to disclose documents, such as minutes of meetings between trustees, which contain this confidential information: *Re Londonderry's Settlement* (1965). A disgruntled beneficiary might, however, bring legal proceedings alleging bad faith, and the confidential documents would then be made available on discovery.

INVESTMENT

Purpose

The investment of trust funds is a major aspect of the administration of trusts and will be a feature of all but the most primitive of trusts. This is particularly so when the subject matter of the trust is money (as opposed to, say, a house).

Investment should be aimed to shield the fund from the depreciating effects of inflation and to generate income for any one with a life interest. It is common practice to insert an express investment clause into the trust instrument. The trustee's ability to invest is also subject to statutory regulation in the form of the **Trustee Act 2000**.

Statutory Obligations

Unless the trust instrument contains an express investment clause, the duty to invest is now widened and regulated by Pt II of the **Trustee Act 2000**. This duty is designed to ensure that the trustees treat income and capital beneficiaries in an impartial manner. This might be described as a duty to act fairly between all beneficiaries. As Hoffmann J. admitted in *Nestlé v National Westminster Bank Plc* (1988), "The trustees must act fairly in making investment decisions which may have different consequences for different classes of beneficiaries". It is also intended to minimise risk while the trustees achieve a reasonable return on the capital invested.

General power

Section 3 offers the trustee a general power of investment and authorises "any kind of investment that he could make if he were absolutely entitled to the assets of the trust". An investment for these purposes requires an anticipation of profit or income (e.g. granting a mortgage on terms that it will be repaid with interest). This rids the law of the authorised categorisations previously set out in the (now repealed) Trustee Investments Act 1961. Section 8 gives the trustee the general power to acquire land whether or not it is designed to generate a rental income. It might be used, for example, to provide a home for a beneficiary.

Suitability

Section 4 requires the trustees, when making an investment, to have regard to the suitability of particular investments and the need for diversification. These are described as the standard investment criteria. As the trustees are required to add diversity to their investment portfolio, they have to be judged on overall performance and not the failure or success of a particular investment: *Nestlé v National Westminster Bank Plc* (1988). Of course, the trustees must carry out periodic reviews of their investment portfolio and, if necessary, vary the investments.

Advice

Section 5 requires the trustees to obtain and consider investment advice from a suitable source. The source could be an expert trustee or an outside adviser. This rule gives way when it would be reasonable to proceed without such advice (e.g. if the investment is small). Trustees are not obliged to follow the advice received, but if they decline to do so they run the risk of being liable for any resultant loss.

Trustee's Duty of Care

Portfolio theory

At common law, the duty of care placed upon a trustee when investing trust funds was higher than that imposed on him when carrying out his other administrative functions. The general yardstick was that that the trustee must invest the trust property wisely, acting as an ordinary prudent man making investments: *Learoyd v Whiteley* (1886). This accepts that a prudent man of business might still invest in risky ventures. This test was, however, to prove ill-suited to developing investment practices and it became relatively meaningless. In *Nestlé v National Westminster Bank Plc* (1988), the modern **portfolio theory** was launched. This entails that, as trustees will often introduce an element of diversity to their investment portfolio, they are to be judged on their overall performance and not on the failure or success of a particular investment.

Expected standards

The standard of care expected of a trustee has been redefined in s.1 of the **Trustee Act 2000**. This overhauled duty is not limited merely to investment and extends widely to most functions carried out by a trustee. The standard of care prescribed in the **2000 Act** confirms that a professional trustee is expected to show a higher degree of care than a lay trustee. As evident from *Bartlett v Barclays Bank Trust Co Ltd* (1980), a trust company with specialist staff will be judged on a different level to an unpaid, family trustee. Subject to exclusion in the trust instrument, s.1 provides that the trustee must exercise such care and skill as is reasonable in the circumstances having regard:

- to any special knowledge or experience that he has or holds himself out as having. This instils a subjective element into the test; and
- if he acts as trustee in the course of a business or profession, to any special knowledge or experience that it is reasonable to expect of a person acting in the course of that business or profession. This instils an objective element into the test.

Non-Financial Considerations

The duty of a trustee is to act in the best financial interests of the beneficiaries. This entails that the trustee must obtain the best rate of return available coupled with diversification of risks. This is so even where it is against the political, social or moral views of some of the beneficiaries. In *Cowan v Scargill* (1985), the investment policy of the mineworkers' pension fund was challenged. The dispute concerned investments in foreign energy companies. Some trustees objected on the ground that these companies were in direct competition with the domestic mining industry. The High Court held that the trustees had to act in the best financial interests of the beneficiaries and, hence, that they would be in breach of duty if they failed to invest in the overseas energy companies. The trustees had to put aside their personal interest and views.

Ethical investment

It is important to appreciate that ethical investment is not prohibited by the decision in *Cowan*. It is still possible for the trust instrument to sanction ethical investment or to prohibit investment in certain companies. The beneficiaries, moreover, may collectively sanction such an investment policy and the trustees retain the ability to choose ethical investing when the financial returns will be equivalent to an alternative, "non-ethical" portfolio. As regards charitable trusts, however, a modified approach is adopted. The trustees are entitled to decline investments that run contrary to the objectives of that trust (e.g. investing in armament companies): *Harries v Church Commissioners for England* (1992). Examples include cancer research companies and tobacco shares or trustees of temperance societies and brewery and distillery shares. Nevertheless, as demonstrated in the Harries case, charitable trustees are not allowed to pursue a blanket policy of ethical investment if this would be detrimental to value of the trust fund.

Revision Checklist

You should now know and understand:

- **the meaning and role of a "fiduciary";**
- **the various duties that exist when taking office;**
- **the various duties which prevent profit–making by a trustee;**
- **the limited exceptions to the non-profit making rule;**
- **the duty to invest and the statutory safeguards imposed.**

QUESTION AND ANSWER

The Question

Tony and Amy are the trustees of a family trust, the major asset in which is Motor Ltd, a private family company operating four retail garages. By virtue of their office as trustee, Tony and Amy are also directors of Motor Ltd and as such each receives a salary of £80,000 pa. They also each have an option to purchase further shares in Motor Ltd at an advantageous price.

Subsequently, Mend a Car Ltd provides Tony with investment advice and information about a possible purchase of another garage which seems advantageous to the trust. Tony and Amy decide that the trust should proceed with the purchase, but there are insufficient free assets to raise the purchase price of £900,000. Consequently, Amy puts in £500,000 of her own money to complete the purchase. She agrees with Tony that, if the value of the new garage increases, she will take a quarter share of the profit. Within six months the value of the new garage has increased to £1 million.

Advise the beneficiaries of the trust.

Advice and the Answer

This problem question focuses upon the fiduciary duties of the trustees (in this example, Tony & Amy). The answer should start by a description of the special types of relationship that give rise to this duty of loyalty and fidelity. The central theme is that, unless authorised by the trust instrument, the trustee/fiduciary should not profit from his position. Obviously, Tony & Amy are in breach of their fiduciary duties.

First, as regards the salaries of £80,000 each, both are clearly in breach of duty and must account for these sums to the beneficiaries. The answer should consider and discuss case law illustrations (e.g. *Williams v Barton*; *Re Macadam*) and note that this is not a situation where they were appointed independently of the trust (cf. *Re Gee*).

Secondly, the option to purchase shares in Motor Ltd (unless given in the Trust Instrument) also contravenes the trustees' fiduciary duty. This is illustrated by *Keech v Sandford* which demonstrates that a trustee may not put himself in a position where his duty to the trust and his personal interest potentially conflict. It might be that the option is not in the best interests of the trust and it might be that decisions taken by Tony & Amy will promote self interest at the expense of the interests of the beneficiaries. In addition, as the company is trust property the transaction appears to contravene the self-dealing rule and the purchase would then be voidable at the behest of the beneficiaries: *Ex p Lacey*.

Thirdly, the purchase of the garage, while made in good faith and because the trust did not have enough funds, is a breach of trust by Amy. This is illustrated generally by *Keech v Sandford*, but more specifically by cases such as Cooley; Regal Hastings and *Boardman v Phipps*. She will have to account for any profit made on the transaction. The facts that the trust could not otherwise have purchased the garage and that it made a profit are irrelevant.

Powers of Maintenance, Advancement and Delegation

15

INTRODUCTION

As well as labouring under the duties imposed by the trust instrument, the common law and statute, the trustees will have a variety of fiduciary powers (or discretions). A number of powers are conferred by statute whereas others may be stated expressly in the trust instrument. Although for the purposes of this chapter only the powers of maintenance, advancement and delegation will be considered in detail, it is useful to provide an indication of the other powers possessed by trustees.

EXAMPLES

PART II OF THE TRUSTEE ACT 1925 OFFERS TO THE TRUSTEE THE
FOLLOWING POWERS:
- the power to sell the whole or a part of the property at public auction: s.12;
- the power to give a purchaser a good receipt for money paid (except when the property is land in which case the receipt must be by at least two trustees or a trust corporation): s.14;
- the power to compound liabilities by, for example, the payment of debts, accepting security for debts, allowing time for payment of debts and compromising or settling any debt: s.15;
- the power to raise money by the sale or mortgage of trust property: s.16; and
- the power to insure trust property: s.19

MAINTENANCE

DEFINITION CHECKPOINT

Maintenance is to do with the trustees using trust income to provide for the maintenance or benefit of a minor beneficiary. The trustees' power to do so may arise expressly from the trust instrument or under statute.

An Express Power

At common law, there is no general power that allows trustees to divert trust money to provide for the welfare and education of an infant beneficiary. Hence, it became common practice for the trust instrument expressly to give the trustees a power to apply income for maintenance purposes. In such cases, the trustees enjoy the discretion whether or not to make an award. The trustees must, therefore, honestly decide whether or not to exercise the power and make the payment to the parent or guardian of the minor. Some key observations may be made concerning the exercise of an express power to maintain.

Decision making

In reaching their decision, the trustees must have regard to the interests of the minor and not take on board the interests of the settlor or anyone else (e.g. the infant's parents). The trustees have to make a separate decision each time that payment is claimed or made. In *Wilson v Turner* (1883), the trustees handed over the entire income of the trust fund to the father during the infancy of the minor beneficiary without periodically considering the continuing merits of the minor's claim. The money was recoverable from the father's estate. The trustees cannot decide upon a blanket refusal ever to make a maintenance payment. If they do so, a beneficiary can apply to court for an appropriate order.

The Statutory Power

The statutory power of maintenance is to be found in s.31 of the **Trustee Act 1925** which offers trustees a broad, discretionary power to apply trust income for the benefit of a minor (but not an adult) beneficiary. In the light of this statutory power, an express power is no longer necessary or common. Unfortunately, s.31 is notoriously difficult to navigate.

Section 31(1)

This provides that, "trustees may, at their sole discretion, pay to his parent or guardian, if any, or otherwise apply for or towards his maintenance, education or benefit, the whole or such part of the income of that property as may, in all the circumstances, be reasonable . . .". Trustees, therefore, could pay school fees directly to the school. If trustees are aware of another trust fund available for the maintenance of the minor, a principle of proportionality applies. This entails that, as far as is practicable and unless the court directs otherwise, a proportionate part of each fund should be used for maintenance purposes. The trustees of the respective funds should, if possible, reach agreement concerning the proportion to be paid from each fund.

Exclusion

The statutory power can be modified or excluded, whether expressly or by implication. For example, in *Re Delamere's ST* (1984) the trustees were expressly given an absolute discretion which was not subject to the statutory temperance by the concept of reasonableness. The use of the word "absolutely" sufficed to displace the operation of s.31. In *Re Erskine's ST* (1971), the settlor made provision for the income to be accumulated. This provision demonstrated an intention to exclude the s.31 power to maintain.

Entitlement to income

The s.31 power requires that the trust interest carries the entitlement to intermediate income (i.e. income generated between the date that the gift is made and the date that it vests in the beneficiary). For example, a trust of shares for John if he reaches the age of 18 will vest only when John reaches majority age. In the intervening period, he has a contingent interest. Whether or not the trust was created inter vivos (i.e. a lifetime trust) or by will, John will be entitled to any intermediate income (i.e. the dividends) and can, therefore, benefit from the statutory power to maintain.

The general rule

Subject to a contrary intention, vested gifts or contingent gifts will carry the intermediate income. The exception to the general rule concerns what is known as a contingent pecuniary testamentary disposition. This will not usually carry the right to income. Take, for example, a legacy of £100,000 to John when he reaches 18. As this is a pecuniary legacy (i.e. purely monetary), it attracts income only when it becomes payable and not during the intervening period. Hence, John is not entitled to the income.

Maintenance, education or benefit

Section 31 is not restricted to run-of-the-mill living expenses and may be used to finance the purchase of a house in which the minor beneficiary can live, or a share in a business partnership for the minor. It can also include the payment of the beneficiary's debts. Income may be employed to pay past maintenance expenses and might even be used to make donations to charity. The money can be employed also for school fees and medical expenses and might be properly used to provide a holiday for the minor.

Making the decision

Section 31(1) directs the trustees to "have regard to the age of the infant and his requirements and generally to the circumstances of the case, and in particular to what other income, if any, is applicable for the same purposes". The trustees must focus upon the best interests of the minor beneficiary and these will vary according to the age of the minor and his family circumstances. Provided that the trustees act in a bona fide and prudent manner, and periodically direct their minds to whether or not the power should be exercised, the court will not interfere.

Ceasing to be a minor

When the beneficiary acquires a vested interest (in income or capital) on attaining 18 years there is no problem. The now adult beneficiary becomes entitled to the unused income. Problems might arise when, on reaching majority age, the beneficiary's interest has still not vested. To assist the beneficiary, s.31(1)(ii) obliges the trustees to pay the income to the beneficiary until his interest either vests or fails. This provision accelerates the beneficiary's interest, as he would not otherwise be entitled to the income until the contingency was satisfied. This assistance is unavailable when there is a direction in the trust instrument to the contrary. For example, in *Re McGeorge* (1963), the testator bequeathed land to his daughter. The bequest was not to take effect until after his wife's death. The 21-year-old daughter claimed the income. The court held that she was not entitled to maintenance from the income because the gift was deferred. This deferral indicated a contrary intention.

ADVANCEMENT

> ### DEFINITION CHECKPOINT
>
> Whereas maintenance concerns a trustee's ability to use trust income to promote the welfare of a minor beneficiary, advancement caters for the use of part of the trust capital to benefit permanently a minor or adult beneficiary before his entitlement under the trust has vested. The key distinction between the two powers, therefore, lies with the source of the funds given to the beneficiary. Other differences are that advancement is not geared to the age of the intended recipient and is designed primarily to make particular, permanent and substantial long term provision for a beneficiary rather than to meet the payment of day-to-day expenses. The trustee's ability to make advance payments from capital will arise either from an express power in the trust instrument or under s.32 of the **Trustee Act 1925**.

ILLUSTRATIONS OF HOW THE POWER OF ADVANCEMENT HAS BEEN
UTILISED INCLUDE:

- buying premises for a beneficiary to set up business;
- providing a dowry on the marriage of a female beneficiary;
- paying the beneficiary's emigration costs;
- discharging the beneficiary's debts;
- financing improvements to land; and
- minimising the beneficiary's tax liability.

An Express Power

A power to apply capital for the advancement or benefit of a minor or contingent beneficiary may be afforded expressly by the trust instrument. An express power might be employed where the settlor regards the statutory power of advancement to be too limited. An express power might also be used to overcome problems of classifying what expenditure should properly come from income and what should come from capital. Take, for example, routine repairs carried out to a beneficiary's house. The cost of such repairs should be defrayed from income (i.e. via the power of maintenance). Nevertheless, it is open to the settlor to provide expressly that this expenditure be made from capital.

The Statutory Power

Section 32 of the **Trustee Act 1925** provides that, subject to the finding of a contrary intention, every trust created after 1925 offers the trustees an absolute discretion to apply capital money for the advancement or benefit of a beneficiary. It does not matter whether the trust is inter vivos or testamentary in nature. The use of the word benefit widens the scope of the power to make payments. The statutory power arises even if there is a possibility that the beneficiary's interest may be defeated: s.32 of the Trustee Act 1925. There are five limitations to the operation of s.32.

Half-share rule

Section 32(1)(a) imposes what is known as the half-share rule. This entails that the money advanced cannot exceed, "altogether in amount one-half of the presumptive or vested share or interest of that person in the trust property". For example, where John is entitled to £100,000 on reaching 35 years of age, the maximum amount in total that can be advanced under s.32 is capped at £50,000.

Capital
Section 32 allows the trustees to make payments only out of "capital". "Capital" for these purposes is limited to personalty (e.g. money and securities) and realty that is subject to a trust of land under the **Trusts of Land and Appointment of Trustees Act 1996**. Its meaning does not extend to settled land or the proceeds of sale of settled land.

Deductible
Section 32(1)(b) imposes an obligation on the beneficiary to account for money advanced when he "becomes absolutely and indefeasibly entitled to a share in the trust property". This means that the money advanced is to be deducted from the beneficiary's eventual share under the trust. This is sometimes known as hotchpot and is designed to ensure equality of distribution between the beneficiaries.

Section 32(1)(c) provides that no payment shall be made to prejudice any interest prior to that of the beneficiary's interest. For example, where property is held on trust for John for life with remainder to Ann. If sums from capital were advanced to Ann while John was still alive, it would reduce the fund from which John's income was to be derived. It would, thereby, prejudice the prior interest of John.

Contrary intention
Section 32 gives way in the face of a contrary intention. In *Re Evans' Settlement* (1967), the trust instrument stated that the trustees were to have a power to advance capital up to a specified amount. As this contradicted the statutory half-share rule, the intention was that s.32 was not to apply.

Discretion
Trustees have to take especial care to ensure that their discretion is exercised properly. In *Simpson v Brown* (1864), a beneficiary successfully recovered from his trustee money that had been advanced to provide the beneficiary with an apprenticeship with a chemist. The chemist was unqualified and unable to provide the beneficiary with the appropriate training. Nevertheless, a trustee who could show that the advancement was to alleviate a need of the beneficiary would generally be shielded. Different considerations apply, however, when the advancement is instead to confer a benefit. More is then expected from a trustee making an advance. The trustees are expected to take on board all relevant considerations and determine that it is a proper case for advancement. The court can, therefore, prevent trustees from an exercise of discretion that is wrong or unreasonable.

Continuing Supervision

Once the discretion to make an advance has been exercised, the trustees must ensure that the funds advanced are actually used for the purposes stated by the beneficiary. In *Re Pauling's ST* (1963), the trustees advanced numerous capital sums to beneficiaries. Although supposedly for the benefit of the beneficiaries, the capital was really used to finance the luxurious lifestyle of their parents. The children were of full age and did not complain about the manner in which the money was used. It was presumed, however, that they were under the undue influence of their parents. The children succeeded in suing the trustees for breach of trust in making improper advances. The Court of Appeal concluded that the power had been improperly exercised and that, as the payments had been made for a particular purpose, the trustees had an obligation to inquire as to the actual use of the money.

DELEGATION

General Rule

The duty of personal service is that a trustee cannot delegate his trust powers and duties: *Speight v Gaunt* (1883). The stance is that a trustee is likely to have been chosen for his personal qualities and wisdom. Hence, and in the absence of an express power given in the trust instrument, a trustee cannot delegate his discretion to select who is to get what under a discretionary trust or as to how the trust fund is to be invested. Nevertheless, there are exceptions to the general rule.

Use of Agents

A trustee can delegate ministerial and administrative functions where special skills are required. A stockbroker might be employed to buy and sell shares or a solicitor to undertake conveyancing work. The power to appoint agents is now governed by the **Trustee Act 2000**. Under s.11, there is a general power that allows trustees to delegate their functions to an agent (including one of themselves, but not a beneficiary).

Not all functions

The **2000 Act**, however, makes some functions incapable of statutory delegation. These are:

* any function concerning whether, or in what manner, the assets of the trust should be distributed;
* the power to decide whether the payment of fees should be made out of capital or income;

Figure 16

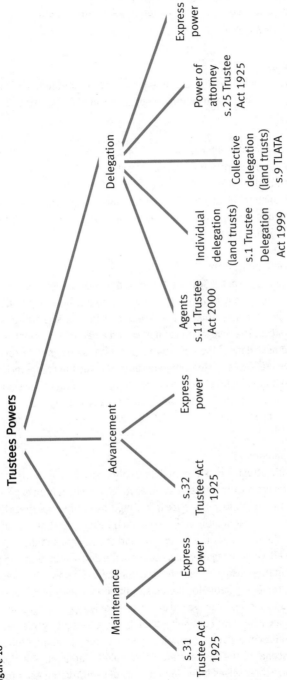

Trustees Powers

- Maintenance
  - s.31 Trustee Act 1925
  - Express power
- Advancement
  - s.32 Trustee Act 1925
  - Express power
- Delegation
  - Agents s.11 Trustee Act 2000
  - Individual delegation (land trusts) s.1 Trustee Delegation Act 1999
  - Collective delegation (land trusts) s.9 TLATA
  - Power of attorney s.25 Trustee Act 1925
  - Express power

- any power to appoint a new trustee; and
- any power capable of delegation under the trust instrument or another statutory provision.

And charities

As regards a charitable trust, a different approach is adopted. The general rule is that there can be no delegation except as provided for by s.11(3). This allows the delegation of:

- purely ministerial functions in carrying out decisions already made;
- any function relating to the investment of assets subject to the trust; and
- any function relating to the raising of funds for the trust (otherwise than by means of profits of a trade carried on by the charity as an integral part of its purpose).

Short-term Delegation

Under section 25(1) of the **Trustee Act 1925**, a trustee can formally (by power of attorney) delegate any or all of his individual duties, powers and discretions vested in him as trustee. This applies whether the trustee is a sole trustee or one of joint trustees. The delegation cannot exceed a period of 12 months from the commencement date of the power. This provision is designed to cater for the situation where, say, a trustee emigrates abroad or the trust property is situated on foreign shores. There are no restrictions upon the number of delegations that can occur and, since the Trustee Delegation Act 1999, delegation can be made in favour of anyone, including an existing trustee and a trust corporation.

After s.25 delegation

The delegating trustee must, at the latest within seven days of the formal delegation, provide the other trustees and anyone else who has an express power to appoint new trustees with notice in writing. The notice must state the terms of the formal delegation: its commencement date and duration, the identity of the donee, the reason for the delegation and the powers and discretions that are delegated. Once delegation has occurred, the donee is in the same position as the delegating trustee, except that the donee has no power to delegate. The delegating trustee is liable for the acts of the donee as if they were his own acts. Section 25 is seldom invoked and is used only when delegation is essential. This is because of the continuing liability of the delegating trustee. Instead, trustees prefer collectively to appoint agents to undertake their functions. In the latter scenario, the trustees are liable only for an agent's actions if the trustees have themselves failed in their duty of care: **Trustee Act 2000**, s.1.

Indefinite delegation

A further power of delegation arises under s.1 of the **Trustee Delegation Act 1999**. The power operates only where the delegating trustee has a beneficial interest in land held by the trust and when the provision is not excluded in the trust instrument. Put simply, it was designed to cater for an express trust of land where the trustees are also the beneficiaries. Section 1 allows such a trustee to delegate indefinitely all trustee functions, relating to the land and income and proceeds of sale from land, by power of attorney. The delegating trustee remains liable for the actions of the donee, but the s.1 facility is not limited to a 12-month period. Trustees who are not also beneficiaries cannot take advantage of this facility and must delegate under the more restricted s.25 procedures. A trustee who has granted an existing power of attorney under that procedure cannot also take advantage of s.1 of the **1999 Act**.

Advantages of s.1

- it enables a co-owner trustee to delegate without having to comply with the restrictions that apply where a third party trustee holds land (e.g. duty to review);
- it enables a co-owner to make effective provision for the disposal of the land where the co-owner becomes mentally incapable. A lasting power of attorney is available under this provision; and
- it ensures that the donee is able to deal with the proceeds of sale of the land.

Collective Delegation

Section 9(1) of the Trusts of Land (Appointment of Trustees) Act 1996 enables trustees of a trust of land collectively to delegate their powers, including the power of sale, to any beneficiary or beneficiaries of full age entitled with an interest in possession to the trust land. Delegation can only be of powers relating to land and not other trust property. The delegation must be by power of attorney given by all the trustees. It cannot, however, be a "lasting power of attorney" which deals with permanent delegation when a trustee is mentally incapable. The power of attorney may be revoked subsequently by any one of the trustees. It ceases also on the appointment of a new trustee.

After s.9 delegation

The delegation may be made for any period of time or indefinitely. Beneficiaries, to whom the powers have been delegated, have the same duties and liabilities as the trustees, but are not regarded as trustees for any other purpose. They cannot sub-delegate their functions nor can they receive capital monies so as to overreach the equitable interest of any beneficiary. If the donee subsequently ceases to be a person beneficially interested in the land (e.g. his interest is bought out), his ability to exercise powers under the delegation also ceases.

You should now know and understand:

- the meaning of maintenance, advancement and delegation;
- the scope and operation of the s.31 power of maintenance;
- the power of advancement conferred by s.32;
- the ability of trustees to delegate their functions.

QUESTION AND ANSWER

The Question

By his will, Zac left his estate on trust to be divided equally between his two daughters, Ann and Beth, on their becoming 18 years of age. Zac died last month when Ann was 14 years of age and Beth was 17 years old.

Ann, who attends a private school, is unsure how her school fees for next year are to be paid. Beth, a newly trained stylist, has the rare opportunity to purchase a successful hairdressing business in a local shopping mall. Both ask their trustee, Calum for financial assistance from the trust fund.

Advise Calum.

Advice and the Answer

This question is about the trustee's powers of maintenance and advancement. The former represents the ability to pay income of the trust for the maintenance, education or benefit of an infant beneficiary (i.e. Ann). The latter concerns the power of the trustee to provide a beneficiary (i.e. Beth) with funds drawn from the trust capital that she would be entitled to had she reached the specified age (i.e. 18 years). The initial problem is that there does not appear to be an express power given to Calum by Zac which allows such payments. Hence, Calum must rely upon the statutory powers given by s.31 (maintenance) and s.32 (advancement) of the **Trustee Act 1925**. There is no suggestion that the statutory powers have been modified or excluded in Zac's will

As regards Ann, it is to be appreciated that s.31 offers Calum a generous discretionary power to apply trust income for her benefit because she is still a minor. Indeed, the payment of school fees is authorised expressly by s.31 which speaks of "maintenance, education or benefit". Ann is, however, required to show that she in entitled to the intermediate income of the trusts. Put simply, is she (albeit with her sister, Beth) entitled to the income generated between the date the trust is created and the date she attains 18 years of age? There is no doubt that both sisters have what is called "contingent interests" and both are entitled to income. Hence, Calum may lawfully exercise the s.31 power of maintenance. The decision, however, rests with Calum who must (by virtue of s.31(1)) have regard to a variety of factors and promote the best interests of Ann. It is likely that Calum will utilise trust income to pay for Ann's fees.

In relation to Beth, she wishes Calum to exercise his s.32 power of advancement which will entail the use of part of trust capital to benefit her permanently. The buying of a business for the beneficiary clearly falls within the scope of "advancement or benefit" and is use permitted by s.32. There are, however, three factors worth noting here. First, the "half-share rule" limits Beth's share to half of her eventual entitlement under the trust (i.e. here a maximum of 25 per cent of the trust capital can be employed for her advancement). Secondly, when she reaches 18 years, Beth will have to account for the sums advanced. Thirdly, Calum must take care to exercise his discretion in a proper and reasonable manner. This entails that he must take into account all relevant circumstances in determining whether this is a suitable instance for the s.32 power to be exercised. If Calum fails to take sufficient care, he can be liable to Beth for the amount advanced: *Simpson v Brown*. Due to Beth's young age, limited business experience and the high costs likely to be involved, this does not appear to be a suitable case for advancement.

Variation of Trusts

16

INTRODUCTION

Until the trust is brought to an end, the trustees must carry out their duties according to the terms of the trust and the rules of equity. As a trust may last for years, however, it is possible that the original terms of the trust may become outmoded and unreasonable. This might occur in relation to the original management and administrative provisions of the trust or the beneficial interests as originally allocated by the settlor. In limited circumstances, the law allows the terms of a trust to be varied.

AN EXPRESS POWER

A variation of the trust terms might be catered for by the settlor giving to the trustees a power to amend the trust. This is a common feature of modern pension trusts. If such ability is given by the trust instrument, the court will be vigilant to ensure that it is properly exercised for the purpose for which it was granted and as intended by the settlor: *Society of Lloyds v Robinson* (1999). Accordingly, any restrictions on the power of amendment must be complied with.

THE RULE IN SAUNDERS V VAUTIER

Provided that they are adult, of sound mind and between themselves entitled absolutely to the trust property, the beneficiaries may unanimously dismantle the trust or vary its terms. This is known as the rule in *Saunders v Vautier* (1841). The purpose of variation is usually to minimise potential tax liabilities. The rule cannot apply, however, where the beneficiaries are children, include persons not yet born, are not all of sound mind or cannot all be found. The rule is not limited merely to fixed trusts and applies also to discretionary trusts: *Re Smith* (1928).

INHERENT JURISDICTION

Generally the court has little power to authorise a departure from the terms of the trust, but a variation can be made under the inherent jurisdiction of the

Figure 17

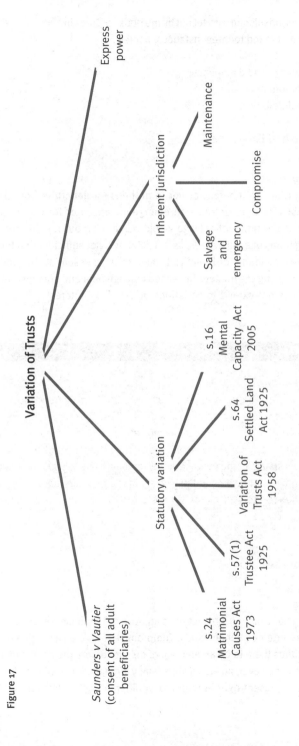

Variation of Trusts

Saunders v Vautier (consent of all adult beneficiaries)

Statutory variation

- s.24 Matrimonial Causes Act 1973
- s.57(1) Trustee Act 1925
- Variation of Trusts Act 1958
- s.64 Settled Land Act 1925
- s.16 Mental Capacity Act 2005

Inherent jurisdiction

- Salvage and emergency
- Compromise
- Maintenance

Express power

court. This jurisdiction was set out by the House of Lords in *Chapman v Chapman* (1954) and limited to three instances, namely:

- salvage and emergency;
- compromise; and
- maintenance.

Salvage and Emergency

Meaning

The court has an inherent power to authorise a departure from the terms of a trust where an unforeseen emergency arises or for the purposes of salvage. An example of salvage would be carrying out repairs to prevent a building from collapsing: *Re Jackson* (1882). It is not sufficient that the repairs are merely desirable or beneficial, they must be essential. The variation is limited to giving the trustees increased management and administration powers. It does not extend to variations of beneficial interests: *Re Tollemache* (1903).

KEY CASE

RE NEW (1901)
A less conventional example of salvage arose from *Re New* (1901). There the trustees held legal title to shares in a particular company and, as an emergency matter, sought to become involved in the capital reconstruction of that company. As a result, the existing shares would be exchanged for new shares in the reconstructed company. This fell outside the trustees' powers of investment as set out in the trust instrument. The court sanctioned the transaction on the basis that it was analogous to the salvage cases.

Compromise

Meaning

The court has a limited jurisdiction to approve compromises on behalf of minors and unascertained beneficiaries. Compromises are given a restricted meaning that requires there to be an element of dispute before the court can interfere. It does not, however, include a mere family arrangement in which a beneficiary gives up a present right in return for a different right: *Chapman v Chapman* (1954).

MASON V FARBROTHER (1983)

In *Mason v Farbrother* (1983), the trustees of a pension fund applied to the court to give them wider powers of investment than they already possessed. There was a dispute concerning the original investment clause, but the court refused to substitute a new investment clause under its inherent jurisdiction. The courts are wary about the possibility of beneficiaries inventing disputes so that the terms of the trust could be varied.

Maintenance

The court may vary a trust so as to award maintenance from income that the testator has directed should be accumulated. For example, the testator may make provision for his family, but might seek to postpone the enjoyment of the gift while the estate is increasing in value. The court will assume that the testator did not intend for his family to go short in the interim period and can override his express directions by ordering the payment of maintenance: *Havelock v Havelock* (1881). Any such order will necessarily result in a variation of the beneficial interests. The jurisdiction is not restricted to urgent cases and maintenance is not limited to minor beneficiaries.

STATUTORY JURISDICTION

The courts are given wider powers to vary the terms of trusts by a variety of statutory provisions.

Section 57(1) of the Trustee Act 1925

This provision permits variation of a trust for the purposes of administration and management. The court can intervene where it is expedient to do so even where there is no emergency. Section 57 gives no power to vary the beneficial interests under a trust: *Re Downshire Settled Estates* (1953). The provisions of the section are deemed to be incorporated into every settlement. The section has been used to authorise the sale of chattels, the sale of land where the necessary consents were refused, the purchase of a residence for the tenant for life and to give wider investment powers.

Section 64(1) of the Settled Land Act 1925

This section deals with the variation of strict settlements. It gives the court power to sanction departures from the trust that are for the benefit of the land or the beneficiaries provided that they could have been effected by an absolute owner.

The section is not limited to management and administration and can be used to alter beneficial interests. Before the enactment of the Variation of Trusts Act 1958, it was often used to minimise tax liability. As, since 1996, no new settlements can be created, this power will eventually become redundant.

Section 24 of the Matrimonial Causes Act 1973

Section 24 allows the High Court, when making an order of divorce or annulment of marriage, to make a property adjustment order. It applies also to registered same-sex partnerships under the **Civil Partnership Act 2004**. Section 24 can operate to vary the trusts contained in any settlement that was made for the benefit of the parties to the marriage or the children of that marriage. This jurisdiction caters for the recasting of beneficial interests. In *Brooks v Brooks* (1999), the husband's pension scheme was varied for the benefit of a divorced wife.

Section 16 of the Mental Capacity Act 2005

Section 16 gives the Court of Protection the power to make a settlement of a patient's property. Section 16(7) allows the court to vary that settlement in such manner as it thinks fit where, prior to the death of the patient, either a material fact has emerged that was not originally disclosed or a substantial change in circumstances has occurred. In *Re CWHT* (1978), the Court of Protection ordered that certain property of a patient be settled on trust. This gave the patient's sister a life interest with remainder for the patient's children and remoter issue. No power of revocation was reserved. Subsequently, the trust was varied during the lifetime of the patient so that the property was to be divided between tenant for life and the remaindermen.

THE VARIATION OF TRUSTS ACT 1958

Background

This Act was passed because of the decision in *Chapman v Chapman* (1954) where the House of Lords refused to vary the beneficial interests of a trust under the court's inherent jurisdiction to compromise claims. The **1958 Act** confers a wide discretionary jurisdiction on the High Court to approve an arrangement varying or revoking all or part of an expressly created private trust. The Act does no more than give the court power to consent to arrangements on behalf of those unable to consent themselves. The trust instrument, moreover, cannot exclude this jurisdiction.

What Variations?

Under the Act, variations can be made covering not only administrative matters, but also beneficial interests, provided always that the arrangement is for the benefit of the person on whose behalf the court is giving approval. Indeed, the Act has been used for a variety of purposes, including inserting a power of advancement, terminating an accumulation and inserting an accumulation period. It is, however, most often used to achieve tax savings. Trustees should make an application only if they believe that the variation will benefit the beneficiaries and there is no adult beneficiary prepared to make an application. The beneficiaries should be unanimous. If not, the non-consenting beneficiaries should be joined as defendants.

On Whose Behalf?

The statutory list
The persons on whose behalf the court may approve a variation are set out in s.1(1) of **1958 Act** and are:

* any person who by reason of infancy or other incapacity is incapable of assenting. This is a straightforward classification that embraces those too young to consent and those of unsound mind who cannot consent;
* any person unborn. Such beneficiaries obviously cannot consent to a variation;
* any person who has a discretionary interest under a protective trust. Put simply, this caters for the variation of protective trusts;
* any person who may become entitled to an interest under the trust at a future date or on the happening of a future event. Put simply, this covers those with a mere expectation of entitlement under the trust. Section 1 goes on to exclude, "any person who would be of that description, or a member of that class, as the case may be, if the said date had fallen or the said event had happened at the date of the application to the court".

KEY CASE

RE SUFFERT'S ST (1961)
Re Suffert's ST (1961) offers a good example of the last category of person. There a spinster was entitled to the income under a protective trust. After her death, the property was destined to go to her statutory next of kin (three cousins). She sought a variation under which a fund of £500 would be held on trust for her cousins with the remainder of the fund (some £8,300) to be held on trust for herself absolutely. One cousin consented to the application, but the others did not. She invited the court to approve the arrangement on behalf of the other two cousins as well as any unborn or unascertained persons who might become entitled. Buckley J. held

that, while he could approve the variation on behalf of the unborn and the unascertainable, the court could not approve the arrangement on behalf of the two cousins. The cousins would have been entitled as next of kin had the tenant for life been dead at the date of the court application and, therefore, they fell within the prescribed exception. The cousins had themselves to decide whether or not to consent.

Benefit

With the exception of discretionary beneficiaries under protective trusts, the arrangement must be for the benefit of the persons on whose behalf approval is sought. Although most cases concern a financial (particularly tax) advantage, this is not the only factor that the courts will consider. The variation must be for the overall benefit of those on whose behalf the application is made.

KEY CASES

RE REMNANT'S ST (1970), RE CL (1969) AND RE WESTON'S SETTLEMENTS (1969)

- In *Re Remnant's ST* (1970), the removal of a forfeiture provision, activated on becoming or marrying a Roman Catholic, was a benefit as its retention could cause trouble within the family. This was so even though the change would be financially detrimental to the beneficiaries.
- In *Re CL* (1969), a Mental Health Act patient sacrificed her life interest, for no consideration, for the benefit of her daughters. There was no financial advantage for her personally. The benefit was a moral one. The court was influenced by the fact that her income greatly exceeded her outgoings, that she was unlikely ever to be discharged from care and that this is what she would have wished for had she been of full mind.
- In *Re Weston's Settlements* (1969), the settlor sought approval of an arrangement under which property settled on his sons would be transferred from the existing English settlements to settlements based in the Channel Isles. The purpose was to avoid capital gains tax in the region of £163,000. The drawback was that the settlor's sons would have to take up residence in the Channel Isles. It was not for the benefit of the children to be uprooted from England and transported to another country simply to avoid tax.

You should now know and understand:

- **the inherent jurisdiction of the court to vary trusts;**
- **the various statutory means by which trusts may be varied;**
- **the purpose of the Variation of Trusts Act 1958;**
- **how the 1958 Act operates.**

QUESTION AND ANSWER

The Question

Explain the circumstances in which a trust may be varied.

Advice and the Answer

Absent an express power in the trust instrument, the general rule is that a departure from the terms of the original trust is not permissible even if it would be in the interests of the beneficiaries: *Chapman v Chapman*. As with all general rules, however, there are exceptions. It is these exceptions that must be discussed and explained. Accordingly, the essay must explore the various statutory provisions which facilitate variation, the inherent (albeit limited) jurisdiction of the court to vary a trust for the purposes of salvage and emergency, compromise an maintenance and the ability of the adult beneficiaries of sound mind unanimously to vary the terms of the trust.

As regards the statutory powers of variation, the following must be considered:

i) s.57(1) of the Trustee Act 1925 which allows for variations concerning the administration and management of the trust (e.g. to facilitate the sale of trust property);

ii) s.64(1) of the Settled Land Act 1954 which caters for the variation of strict settlements which are for the benefit of the trust and which could have been made by an absolute owner. This includes a variation of beneficial interests;

iii) s.24 of the Matrimonial Causes Act 1973 which permits the variation of existing family trusts on divorce or annulment of marriage so as to enable a property adjustment order to be made;

iv) s.16(7) of the Mental Capacity Act 2005 permits the Court of Protection to vary the terms of a trust of a patient's property when a material fact has emerged or a substantial change of circumstances has occurred;

v) s.1 of the Variation of Trusts Act 1958 which offers the court wide powers to vary trusts for the benefit of those who are unable to consent themselves (e.g. infants, unborn persons and those with a future interest). This could include the removal of a forfeiture provision on marrying a Roman Catholic *(Re Remnant's ST)* or the sacrifice of a life interest in favour of an incapacitated person's daughters *(Re CL)*. There must, moreover, be some benefit (whether financial or moral) before the variation can be made *(Re Weston's Settlements)*.

The answer must then consider the limited inherent jurisdiction of the court to vary trusts as illustrated in *Chapman v Chapman*. This arises, first, in salvage and emergency cases where the trustees require additional managerial and administrative powers (e.g. where a trust building is in severe disrepair: *Re Jackson*). Secondly, it emerges in cases where a real dispute is to be compromised (*Mason v Farbrother* dispute as to construction of an investment clause). Thirdly, it can operate in cases where maintenance from trust income is sought for the settlor's family (*Havelock v Havelock*).

The final aspect to be discussed is the rule in *Saunders v Vautier*. This case contains the sensible rule that a variation can occur with the consent of all the beneficiaries who have reached the age of majority and are of sound mind. If one beneficiary is a minor or incapacitated, the rule cannot operate. Instead, an application should be made under the **Variations of Trust Act 1958**.

Breach of Trust and Associated Remedies

....

17

INTRODUCTION

A trustee assumes a range of duties and responsibilities, breach of which exposes him to liability in an action by the beneficiary. The trustee has a liability either to compensate for loss or to account for gains subsequent to the breach. The essential principle is the same whether the trust is express or implied. Not surprisingly, the beneficiaries have a number of remedies against the trustee and sometimes third parties for a breach of trust. This Chapter focuses on possible breaches of duty and the range of remedies that a beneficiary may pursue of both a personal and proprietary nature. A trustee may be liable for both acts of omission (failing to do what he ought to do) and acts of commission (doing what he should not do). There are many examples of breach in a variety of different circumstances. It is difficult, therefore, to lay down any exhaustive list of possible breaches that will give rise to trustee liability.

Categories of Breach
Nevertheless, breaches of trust by a trustee fall within three broad categories:

- gaining an unauthorised profit;
- failing to act with care and skill in the administration of the trust; and
- misapplications of trust property.

....

LIABILITY FOR BREACH

Liability of a Trustee for His Own Acts
If the trustee commits a breach of trust, he is liable to the trust for any loss incurred or personal gain made. In the case of an unauthorised investment, he is liable for the loss incurred when it is sold: *Knott v Cottee* (1852). Where the trustee wrongfully retains an unauthorised investment, he is liable for the difference between the price he obtains when it is sold and the price that would

have been obtained had he sold it at the right time: *Fry v Fry* (1859). Where a trustee improperly realises an authorised investment, he must replace it or pay the difference between the price obtained and the cost of repurchasing the investment: *Phillipson v Gatty* (1848). Where the court has to assess the cost of replacing the investment, it will be valued at the date of judgment: *Re Bell's Indenture* (1980).

Former trustees

A trustee is not, however, liable for breaches of trust committed by his predecessors. He should, nevertheless, sort out any irregularities he discovers when taking office, including obtaining satisfaction from the old trustees. If the trustee fails to do so, he may himself be liable for loss arising from this omission. If the trustee takes the appropriate steps on appointment, he is entitled to assume that there has been no pre-existing breach of trust.

Retirement

On retirement, a trustee (or, if he is deceased, his estate) will still remain liable for breaches of trust that occurred during his stewardship. Generally, a trustee is not liable for breaches committed by his successors unless his retirement occurred so that the breach could be committed or to avoid his becoming involved with it: *Head v Gould* (1898).

Liability for Acts of Co-Trustees

Scope

A trustee can never be vicariously liable for the acts of another trustee. Liability can, however, arise when the trustee himself is at fault in allowing another trustee to commit a breach. The yardstick is whether the "innocent" trustee acted as a prudent man of business and is not limited to acts of wilful default. A trustee will be liable for a breach of trust resulting from the act or omission of a co-trustee in the following situations:

- leaving trust income in the hands of a co-trustee for too long without making proper inquiries: *Townley v Sherborne* (1634);
- concealing a breach committed by his fellow trustees: *Boardman v Mossman* (1779); and
- standing by while to his knowledge a breach of trust is being committed (*Booth v Booth* (1838)) or contemplated (*Wilkins v Hogg* (1861)).

Joint and Several Liability

Meaning

Where two or more trustees are each liable for a breach of trust, they are jointly and severally liable. This means that any one of the trustees may be sued for the full amount or, if they all are sued, judgment may be executed against any one (or more) of them. At common law, all trustees who were in breach were liable equally and, if one had paid more than his share, he could claim contribution from the others. Under the Civil (Liability) Contribution Act 1978, however, the sums recoverable must be "such as may be found by the court to be just and equitable having regard to the extent of that person's responsibility for the damage in question". It is open to the court, therefore, to depart from the equitable presumption of equal responsibility where the facts of the case demand.

Indemnity from other trustees

There are also circumstances in which a trustee can claim indemnity from one or more of his co-trustees. Indemnity is appropriate where:

- one trustee has acted fraudulently or is alone morally culpable: *Bahin v Hughes* (1886);
- the breach was committed solely on the advice of a solicitor co-trustee: *Head v Gould* (1898);
- only one trustee has benefited from the breach: *Bahin v Hughes* (1886); and
- one of the trustees is also a beneficiary: *Chillingworth v Chambers* (1896).

PROTECTION OF TRUSTEES FROM LIABILITY

Exemption Clauses

Scope

A trust instrument will commonly restrict the liability of a trustee (i.e. by way of an exemption clause). In *Armitage v Nurse* (1997), an express exemption protecting a trustee "from any cause whatsoever unless such loss or damage shall be caused by his own actual fraud" was upheld. This excluded liability for breach of trust in the absence of a dishonest intention on the part of the trustee. There can, therefore, be no exclusion of liability arising from fraud or intentional wrongdoing. As demonstrated in *Walker v Stones* (2000), the concept of "dishonesty" is, however, hard to define.

KEY CASE

BARRACLOUGH V MELL (2005)

In *Barraclough v Mell* (2005), a trustee exemption clause excused the trustee from liability for breach of duty for his own personal acts except when he knew that the relevant acts were wrongful or when he had no belief that the act was right and did not care if it was wrong. The trustee misapplied trust money by paying £64,000 to the wrong beneficiaries. Although the trustee admitted negligence, she still sought to avoid liability under the exemption clause. The High Court concluded that, as she had genuinely thought that she was acting within the terms of the trust, she was protected by the exemption clause.

Reform

The wide use of exclusion clauses entails that the protection afforded to beneficiaries is less strong than it was in the past. This has prompted calls that professional trustees should insure against potential liability rather than hide behind broadly drafted exclusion clauses. In 2003, the Law Commission published a Consultation Paper which provisionally concluded that the present law was unsatisfactory and that professional trustees should not be exempt from liability following a negligent breach of trust. This notion was, however, rejected in Report of the Law Commission, "Trustee Exemption Clauses" (2006). Instead, a rule of practice was recommended under which the trustee must take steps, when the trust is created, to make the settlor aware of the meaning and effect of including an exclusion clause.

Statutory Relief

Section 61

The court is given the discretion to relieve (in whole or in part) a trustee from liability by s.61 of the **Trustee Act 1925**. This discretion arises when the trustee has "acted honestly and reasonably, and ought fairly to be excused for the breach of trust and for omitting to obtain the directions of the court in the matter in which he committed such breach". There are no rules when relief will be granted and each case will be judged on its own particular circumstances: *Re Evans* (1999). The burden of proof lies on the trustee to establish that he acted reasonably and honestly and as prudently as he would have done in organising his own affairs. A paid trustee is expected to exercise a higher standard of diligence and knowledge than an unpaid trustee: s.1 of the **Trustee Act 2000**. Hence, an unpaid trustee is more likely to be released from liability than his professional counterpart.

RE KAY (1897), NATIONAL TRUSTEES CO OF AUSTRALASIA LTD V GENERAL FINANCE CO (1905) AND BARRACLOUGH V MELL (2005)

- In *Re Kay* (1897), the testator left £22,000. The apparent liabilities of the estate were £100. The trustee advertised for creditors of the estate, having previously given the widow £300. It turned out that the testator's debts amounted to more than £22,000. The court held that the trustee had acted honestly and reasonably. It was unforeseeable that the actual debts would be more than £22,000 when the apparent debts were £100.
- In *National Trustees Co of Australasia Ltd v General Finance Co* (1905), the trustees followed the advice of a solicitor which was incorrect. The trust was large and complicated and the court held that the advice of a trust expert, a senior counsel, should have been sought. The trustees did not fall within s.61.
- In *Barraclough v Mell* (2005), the trustee was shielded behind the very wide terms of the exclusion clause. The High Court made clear, however, that it would have refused relief to the trustee under s.61. The trustee's conduct was grossly negligent and, while she had acted honestly, she had not acted reasonably and ought not fairly to be excused for the breach of trust.

Acts of Beneficiaries

General rule

The rule is that a beneficiary who has consented to, or participates in, a breach of trust cannot afterwards sue the trustees for breach of trust. This rule applies when three conditions are satisfied:

- the beneficiary was of full age and sound mind at the time of agreement or concurrence;
- the beneficiary had full knowledge of the relevant facts and of the legal effect of his actions; and
- the beneficiary acted voluntarily and was not under the undue influence of another.

KEY CASES

NAIL V PUNTER (1832) AND RE PAULING'S ST (1964)

- In *Nail v Punter* (1832), the trustees held stock on trust for a woman for life, with remainder to such person as she should by will appoint. Her husband persuaded her to sell the stock in breach of trust. She died and appointed her husband as her beneficiary. It was held that he could not sue the trustees because he had been a party to the breach of trust.
- In *Re Pauling's ST* (1964), a bank was a trustee for a woman for life, with remainder to her children. The bank advanced money to the (now adult) children, but their parents misapplied the funds. The children later sought to recover the money from the trustee bank. As a result of undue influence exerted by their father, the children had not been fully aware of the nature of their entitlements and, therefore, could succeed.

Indemnity from a Beneficiary

The court has an inherent jurisdiction to order that a trustee or other beneficiaries be indemnified out of the interest of a beneficiary who instigated or requested such a breach. If the beneficiary merely concurred in the breach, it must be shown he received a benefit from it: *Montford v Cadogan* (1816). This is supplemented by s.62 of the **Trustee Act 1925** which states:

> "Where a trustee commits a breach of trust at the instigation or request or with the consent in writing of a beneficiary, the court may, if it thinks fit . . . make such order as to the court seems just, for impounding all or any part of the interest of the beneficiary in the trust estate by way of indemnity to the trustee or persons claiming through him".

PERSONAL CLAIMS AGAINST A TRUSTEE

DEFINITION CHECKPOINT

The trustee's liability to account provides the basis for a beneficiary's claim against the trustee in cases of breach of trust. As the trustee is accountable for the stewardship of the trust, it is open to the beneficiary to have the account taken and to require the trustee to restore the trust fund or compensate for any deficiency arising through the trustee's action/inaction.

- The account is surcharged where a trustee is made liable for a breach (such as negligence), which does not involve a misappropriation of trust property. In such cases, the trustee must compensate the trust fund from his own pocket.
- The account is falsified where the trustee has misapplied trust property. In such cases the trustee is required to restore to the trust the specific property, its equivalent or its monetary value to the trust fund.
- In the case of unauthorised profit, the beneficiary may elect not to falsify the account, but to accept or adopt the transaction. Hence, if a profit arises from an unauthorised transaction the beneficiaries can claim it: *Daker v Somes* (1834).

Set-Off Rules

A trustee cannot claim that a profit made in one transaction should be set off against a loss suffered in another transaction: *Dimes v Scott* (1828). If, however, the gain and loss are part of the same transaction, then the rule against set-off will not apply: *Fletcher v Green* (1864). For example, in *Bartlett v Barclays Bank Trust Co Ltd* (1980) the bank was able to set off the losses on a development project at the Old Bailey against the profits made on another development at Guildford. Both resulted from a policy of unauthorised speculative investments.

Equitable Compensation

Equitable compensation is also payable directly to beneficiaries where there is no need to reconstitute a trust fund, for example, where a beneficiary has become entitled to the entirety of the trust fund but the trustee has misapplied the property. A direct payment from the trustee's pocket to the beneficiary is deemed to be by way of equitable compensation to the beneficiary. The claimant, however, may only recover for loss caused by the defendant's breach: *Target Holdings Ltd v Redfearns* (1996).

TRACING

The Process of Tracing

Meaning

Technically, tracing is not a remedy. Instead, it is a process which identifies any trust property that has passed into the hands of a recipient in breach of trust.

The beneficiary is, thereby, positioned to pursue a remedy that enforces his ownership of that property. At its most simple, a beneficiary may be able to follow the specific property into the hands of the recipient, in which case he will seek a return of that specific property. Following is the process of identifying the same asset as it moves from hand to hand. In the alternative, a substitution of the original trust property may be traced. For example, if money appropriated in breach of trust is used to pay the total purchase price of a number of shares, there has been a substitution of the money for the shares. The beneficiary can then claim the new asset (the shares) as a substitute for the old (the money).

Advantages

Tracing has several advantages over a mere personal claim:

- it may be available where there is no effective personal claim as where the trustee is insolvent and the person who has the property is an innocent volunteer;
- if the person, B, who has the property goes bankrupt, then the owner, A, can claim priority over B's creditors. A is a secured creditor as he has a proprietary claim, i.e. a claim which is attached to the property;
- claimants are entitled to any income produced by the assets that have been traced from the date on which the property came into the defendant's hands. This is in contrast with claims in personam that only carry interest from the date of judgment. In some cases, the claimant will not just be entitled to the return of his money, but also to any increase in the value of the property.

Traditional distinction

Historically, different rules have applied to tracing at common law and in equity. The common law rules are characterised by a restrictive approach. As will become clear, the utility of common law tracing is evident only in delimited circumstances. Judges and commentators alike have voiced regret that the law had failed to develop a single system of rules. For example, in *Jones (FC) & Sons v Jones* (1996), Millett L.J. saw no merit in having distinct and differing tracing rules at law and in equity, "given that tracing is neither a right nor a remedy but merely the process by which the plaintiff establishes what has happened to his property and makes good his claim that the assets which he claims can properly be regarded as representing his property". He reiterated the same point in *Foskett v McKeown* (2001). Nevertheless, for the time being the distinction remains: *Shalson v Russo* (2003).

Common Law Tracing

Meaning

At common law, tracing the property was possible as long as it was not mixed with other property. Hence, once money is mixed, as in a bank account, there can be no tracing at common law. Thus only identifiable tangible property could be traced, as could a chose in action (e.g. a bank balance) or property purchased with the claimant's money. Tracing into exchanged assets is permissible at common law. In *Taylor v Plumer* (1815), for example, the defendant handed money to his stockbroker to purchase exchequer bonds. The stockbroker purchased American investments instead. On the stockbroker's bankruptcy, the defendant was entitled to the investments that represented the money he had given to the stockbroker.

KEY CASE

JONES (FC) & SONS V JONES (1996)

In *Jones (FC) & Sons v Jones* (1996), the sum of £11,700 was loaned from the partnership account of a firm to the wife of one of the partners. With the money she made a successful stock-market investment. She realised the investment and paid almost £50,000 into a separate bank account. The partnership was, however, deemed to have been bankrupt before the loan payment. The Official Receiver and not the partner's wife was, thereby, entitled to the original £11,700 at the point at which the loan was made. More difficulty surrounded the profits. As there was no fiduciary relationship between the Official Receiver and the wife, and tracing in equity was thereby not possible (see below) the court was left to consider only the common law rules. The Court of Appeal allowed the Official Receiver to recover the profits made on the investment. The common law rules embraced not only the property representing the original, but also the profit made by the defendant's use of it.

Tracing in Equity

Pre-requisites to tracing

For tracing to occur in equity, two conditions must be satisfied:

- there must be a fiduciary relationship between the parties; and
- the property must be traceable.

A fiduciary relationship

The traditional view is that a claimant may take advantage of the equitable tracing rules only if he can demonstrate the existence of fiduciary obligations before the property reaches the recipient's hands: *Agip (Africa) v Jackson* (1990). For the claimant who is a beneficiary under an express trust, for example, this is inevitably straightforward. More difficulty surrounds other types of claims, such as in the case of a mistaken overpayment made by the claimant bank to a recipient bank. In *Chase Manhattan v Israel-British Bank* (1981), therefore, the search for evidence of fiduciary obligations, purely to allow the claimant to trace in equity, led the court to discern a fiduciary duty that arose on the receipt of the payment by the defendant bank when its conscience became duly affected. In *Foskett v McKeown* (2001), Lord Millett admitted that he could see no logical justification for insistence on a fiduciary relationship as a precondition to tracing in equity. It is unclear whether the courts will abandon this requirement at a future time.

The property must be traceable

It may be easy to trace money where it has been invested in shares or channelled into the purchase of property for the wrongdoer. Here, the beneficiary can claim either the property itself or a charge on the property for the money expended in the purchase: *Sinclair v Brougham* (1914). Difficulties arise, however, where money has been placed in a mixed bank account and mingled with other funds. There are various and somewhat complicated rules for dealing with the problem.

Trust funds mixed with trustee's own money

Where a trustee mixes trust funds with his own funds, the rule in *Re Hallett's Estate* (1880) may be applied.

A trustee is presumed to draw on his own money first and is not expected to want to commit a breach of trust. It is only when his own money is exhausted that he is deemed to draw on trust funds. For example: a trustee has £1,000 in an account: £500 of his own funds and £500 of trust funds. He then spends £500 on a holiday. The £500 spent is deemed to be his own money.

Re Hallett's Estate is subject to the overriding principle that the beneficiary has a first charge on any property bought out of a mixed fund. In *Re Oatway* (1903), however, a trustee withdrew money from a mixed fund and invested it. Later he withdrew the rest of the money, which he then dissipated. In such circumstances, the creditors could not successfully claim that the trustee was deemed to spend his own money first. The beneficiaries were, instead, entitled to the investments and any profit made on them.

Lowest intermediate balance

Only the lowest intermediate balance of the account may be traced: *Roscoe v Winder* (1915). To continue with the previous example, £500 of trust money remains in the trustee's personal account. If the trustee dissipates a further £400, but later pays in £200 of his own money, the balance of the account stands at £300. Only £100 may be traced. No part of the £200 added to the account can be deemed to belong to the trustee. The lowest intermediate balance of the account is, therefore, £100. Remember, at all times, the trust property, or its value, must be identifiable as it moves from place to place. Additional value added to the account at a later stage from a different source, will not be deemed to replenish to trust fund: *Bishopsgate Investment Management v Homan* (1995)

Mixture of two trust funds/trust funds mixed with moneys of an innocent volunteer

The rules to deal with more complex mixtures (i.e. two trust funds or a trust fund mixed with the property of an innocent volunteer) are necessarily different so as to balance the competing claims of beneficiaries and innocent volunteers. There are three options:

- first in, first out: *Clayton's Case* (1816). Withdrawals are deemed to occur in the same order in which deposits were made. For example, £500 from Trust A is deposited in a bank account followed by £500 from Trust B, followed by £500 from Trust C. £600 is withdrawn and invested profitably, whereas the remainder in the account is dissipated. Under *Clayton's Case*, Trust A would be entitled to trace £500 into the profitable investment. This allows for a full recovery of the value of the misappropriated funds and a claim to a proportionate share of the profit. Trust B will recover only £100 and the proportion of the profit thereby generated. Trust C recovers nothing. It will come as little surprise that the first in first out rule has attracted criticism;

- proportionality: *Foskett v McKeown* (2001). The method involves a rateable distribution in accordance with amounts contributed to the fund. Where the fund is deficient, all contributors share losses rateably. In the above example, this would work out at £200 of value plus a proportionate share of the profit. This method has the advantages of simplicity and fairness;

- the North American rolling charge: *Barlow Clowes International v Vaughan* (1992). This method has been adopted in the United States and Canada as producing the fairest results. Each deposit and withdrawal affects the overall mixture in the account so that each withdrawal is treated as a withdrawal in the same proportions as the interests in the account bear to each other before the withdrawal is made. Not surprisingly, the rolling charge is difficult and expensive to apply.

Limits to Tracing and Equitable Proprietary Claims

There are a variety of situations where the right to trace is lost or it is clear that the claimant will be unsuccessful. The claimant may fail because:

- property has been consumed, dissipated or destroyed;
- money was paid into an overdrawn account and ceased to be identifiable: *Shalson v Russo* (2003)
- no proprietary claim can be pursued against a bona fide purchaser for value without notice of the equity;
- no claimant can trace who has acquiesced in the wrongful mixing or distribution;
- No tracing will be allowed where it would cause injustice. Accordingly, a "change of position" defence might be accepted if an innocent recipient's position is so changed that he will suffer an injustice if required to repay or to repay in full: *Re Diplock* (1948).

Figure 18

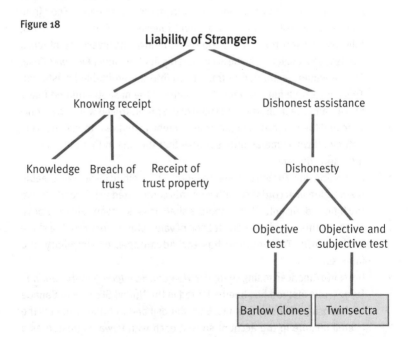

KNOWING RECEIPT AND DISHONEST ASSISTANCE

If a third party has received trust property, but has not retained it, a proprietary remedy is inappropriate. A beneficiary, however, might be able to bring a personal action against the recipient/stranger to the trust if he had received the trust property knowing that it was trust property or assisted in a breach of trust. Equally, where a third party assists, in a dishonest manner, in the misapplication of trust property, he too may be personally liable to account in equity.

Knowing Receipt

> **DEFINITION CHECKPOINT**
>
> Liability to account on the basis of knowing receipt of trust property applies to strangers who receive trust property, or its traceable proceeds, in the knowledge that the property has been misapplied or transferred in breach of trust.

Requirements
The requirements for liability are those identified by Hoffmann L.J. in *El Anjou v Dollar Land Holdings* (1994):

- a disposal of assets in breach of trust or fiduciary duty;
- the receipt by the defendant of assets which are traceable as representing the assets of the claimant; and
- knowledge on the part of the defendant that the assets he received are traceable to a breach of fiduciary duty.

No need for dishonesty
There is no need to show that a recipient is dishonest. Liability will arise only if there is the right type of "knowledge" and the right type of "receipt". A person who receives property innocently, but later discovers that it is trust property, becomes liable to account from that discovery. If the recipient parts with the property before ever knowing that it was trust property, there is no liability.

Traditional categories of knowledge
As to what constitutes knowledge, five categories were identified by Peter Gibson L.J. in the *Baden v Societe General du Commerce SA* (1993):

(i)   actual knowledge;

(ii)   wilfully shutting one's eyes to the obvious;

(iii) wilfully and recklessly failing to make reasonable inquiries;

(iv)   knowledge of circumstances which would indicate the facts to a reasonable man;

(v)   knowledge of facts which would put a reasonable man on inquiry.

Modern interpretations

*   In Re *Montagu's Settlement Trusts* (1987), Megarry V.C. considered the crucial question to be whether the recipient's conscience is sufficiently affected to warrant the imposition of a constructive trust. He qualified knowledge as including not only actual knowledge, but also knowledge of types (ii) and (iii) in the *Baden* case. Megarry V.C. felt it to be doubtful that knowledge of types (iv) and (v) would suffice because the levels of carelessness indicated did not stretch to a want of probity.

*   In *Bank of Credit and Commerce International v Akindele* (2001) Nourse L.J. doubted the use of the *Baden* categories an concluded, "All that is necessary is that the recipient's state of knowledge should be such as to make it unconscionable for him to retain the benefit of the receipt". Unfortunately, Nourse L.J. did not subject his new test to rigorous examination and it remains for future courts to develop its scope and boundaries.

Dishonest Assistance

DEFINITION CHECKPOINT

Where a third party assists in a dishonest manner in the misappropriation of trust property, he may be personally liable in equity to restore the trust fund or compensate for loss occasioned to the trust. Dishonesty on the part of the third party is a sufficient basis of liability, i.e. it is not necessary that the trustee or fiduciary was also acting dishonestly: *Royal Brunei Airlines v Tan* (1995).

Dishonesty

The meaning of dishonesty came before the House of Lords in *Twinsectra Ltd v Yardley* (2002). The majority held that the test for dishonesty was a hybrid (i.e. a combined test) of subjective and objective elements. This entails that a defendant will be personally liable as an accessory if he acted dishonestly by the standards of honest and reasonable people and that he was aware that by those standards he acted dishonestly. Lord Millett (dissenting) opted for a substantially objective test, holding that account should be taken of some subjective elements such as the defendant's actual state of knowledge, but that it is not necessary that he should actually appreciate that he was acting dishonestly.

BARLOW CLOWES INTERNATIONAL LTD (IN LIQUIDATION) V EUROTRUST INTERNATIONAL LTD (2006)

Barlow Clowes International Ltd (in liquidation) v Eurotrust International Ltd (2006), concerned a fraudulent off-shore investment scheme, in which the director of a company providing off-shore services faced an action for dishonest assistance in the misappropriation of investment monies. Although he was deemed dishonest by ordinary objective standards, the Privy Council was required to consider the extent to which his subjective state of mind should be assessed. The director's clear suspicion that monies were misappropriated and conscious avoidance of enquiries that might confirm his suspicions proved sufficient. It was not necessary that he reflect upon normally acceptable standards or, indeed, know all the details as to the trust upon which the money was held. Accordingly, it is not necessary that the defendant knows of the existence of a trust or fiduciary relationship or that the transfer of money involves a breach of either.

Barlow Clowes treats the test for dishonesty as essentially objective. Accordingly, questions remain as to the approach of future courts in interpreting recent decisions and, in particular, the application of the subjective element of the *Twinsectra* test. Indeed, in *Abou-Rahmah v Abacha* (2007), Arden L.J. welcomed the guidance in *Barlow Clowes*, whilst confirming, nonetheless, that that the approach in *Twinsectra* had not been jettisoned. Scope for debate, therefore, remains.

THE PERSONAL ACTION IN RE DIPLOCK

When an executor, in winding up the deceased's estate, wrongfully distributes the estate, a personal action may be brought against the recipient for the overpayment: *Re Diplock* (1948). This personal action is available to an unpaid legatee, creditor or next of kin. It is not available to beneficiaries under an inter vivos (lifetime) trust. In addition, this personal claim is enforceable only to the extent that the money is not recoverable from the negligent executor.

Facts of Re Diplock

The background to *Re Diplock* concerned the will of Caleb Diplock, who gave his residuary estate to "such charitable institutions or other charitable or benevolent objects as my executors may in their absolute discretion select". The executors, thinking this was a valid charitable gift, distributed £203,000 amongst various charities. The next of kin succeeded in their attempt to trace against the charities by establishing a fiduciary relationship between themselves and the executors. There was held to be nothing inequitable in tracing property into the hands of innocent charitable institutions. It was, however, considered to be impracticable to trace funds that had been spent on improving part of a building in the middle of a hospital. Where the charities held the funds without mixing with other funds, all the money was held for the next of kin. Where the money had been mixed the charity and the next of kin shared rateably.

Revision Checklist

You should now know and understand:

- the general rules as to liability for breach of trust;

- how exclusion clauses operate;

- the process of tracing and the circumstances that it can operate at common law and in equity;

- the circumstances that a third party might be liable for knowing receipt and dishonest assistance.

QUESTION AND ANSWER

The Question

Adam was the sole trustee of two trusts: the Village Trust and the Town Trust. Last year, Adam wrongly sold assets belonging to the Village Trust and paid the proceeds of £20,000 into his own bank account, which was £5,000 overdrawn at the time. A month later, Adam paid £3,000 of his own money into the same account. Soon afterwards, a withdrawal of £10,000 from the account was used to purchase shares in City Holdings.

This proved to be a profitable investment. To celebrate, Adam spent £4,000 from the account on a trip to Barbados.

Last month, Adam misappropriated £10,000 from Town Trust and paid this sum into his own bank account. At this stage Adam's account showed a credit balance of £14,000. More recently, Adam has made the following withdrawals:

- he withdrew £5,000 from his account in May and purchased a second hand sports car, which he gave to his girlfriend Brenda. Brenda was very surprised as she knew Adam had no money;
- he withdrew a further £2,000 and gave this to his mum Elsie.

Adam has just died. The shares in City Holdings remain profitable. Brenda has crashed her car, which was uninsured. Elsie has spent the £2,000 on vital repairs to her home. £7,000 remains in Adam's account.

Advise the beneficiaries of Village Trust and Town Trust.

Advice and the Answer

Try to work chronologically through the problem. Adam is the sole trustee of the Village Trust and the Town Trust and, as such, he is in breach of fiduciary duty by virtue of the misappropriation of trust assets. As Adam has died, the beneficiaries of both trusts will seek to trace their equitable interests. Remember, common law tracing is impossible where there are mixed funds (*Agip Africa v Jackson*), but the clear fiduciary relationship between Adam and the Trusts entails that the rules of equitable tracing may be employed.

When Adam wrongly sell the assets of the Village Trust and pays the proceeds into his bank account the balance stands at £15,000. £5,000 is immediately lost to the Village Trust. This is because it cannot trace into an overdrawn account, which is deemed a liability rather than an asset (*Shalson v Russo*).

When Adam adds £3,000 of his own money to the account, he is not deemed to replenish Village Trust value. The Village Trust may trace into the lowest intermediate balance of the account (*Roscoe v Winder*), i.e. £15,000.

£10,000 is then withdrawn for the purchase of City Holding shares. Here *Re Oatway* applies in preference to the rule in *Re Hallett*. As the transaction is profitable, the wrongdoing trustee is not deemed to spend his own money first. The Village Trust can claim the shares and the profit generated.

As regards the £5,000 spent on the holiday, this money is dissipated, the first £3,000 of which is deemed to be Adam's (*Re Hallett*). £4,000 worth of Village Trust assets remain in the account

When £10,000 of Town Trust value is added to the account, the balance stands at £14,000. As the bank account now contains a mixture of two trust funds, different rules come into play to determine the competing claims of both trusts. The courts can apply *Clayton's Case* (first in first out); allow the trusts to share proportionately in profits and losses from the account or apply the rolling charge (*Barlow Clowes*).

Two further withdrawals occur, leaving a balance of £7,000 in the account. The car was a gift to Brenda. A question remains as to the possibility of a personal action by the beneficiaries on the basis of knowing receipt. Did she shut her eyes to the obvious or wilfully and recklessly fail to make the inquiries that an honest and reasonable person would make? Was it unconscionable for her to retain the car (*Akindele*)?

As to Elsie, she seems to be an innocent volunteer. If she cannot show change of position, such that it would be inequitable to permit recovery of trust monies, a charge may be placed on her home to the value of the repairs (*Re Diplock*).

£7,000 remains in the account. Appling *Clayton's Case* would be to the disadvantage of the Village Trust. £4,000 of its value was first into the account before mixing with the Town Trust occurred. Accordingly, the first in first out approach would entail that all the value of Village Trust is lost in the crashed car. The Town Trust would be entitled to the remaining funds in the account. By contrast, rateable sharing for both Trusts would seem to produce a fair outcome, with Village Trust claiming £2,000 and Town Trust the remaining £5,000.

Handy Hints

18

HANDY HINTS

- Equity and trusts is a case law and statute law subject. You have to memorise case names (even if only partially) and statutory provisions and apply them to support your arguments and assertions.
- Always attempt the required number of questions on an examination paper. Try to spread your time evenly and remember more marks may be gained at the beginning of a new question than when finishing off an existing question.
- Read the questions carefully, identify the issues and address them.
- Look at past papers and familiarise yourself with the types of questions that are set.
- Practise hand writing essay and problem style questions (within exam type conditions) and ask your tutor to look over them. Write as clearly as you can and underline the case names that you use so that they stand out. Flow charts and diagrams may help understanding.
- Make sure that you revise sensibly and comprehensively. If you cut your revision down to the bare minimum, you may live to regret it. Remember a topic might not appear at all on the paper or might appear in a form that you find difficult.
- Keep calm both during the revision period and the examination itself.

Index